Voyage of Prayer

― 祈りの旅 ―

HAYATO IMANISHI

SEISEISHA

to the world's end....

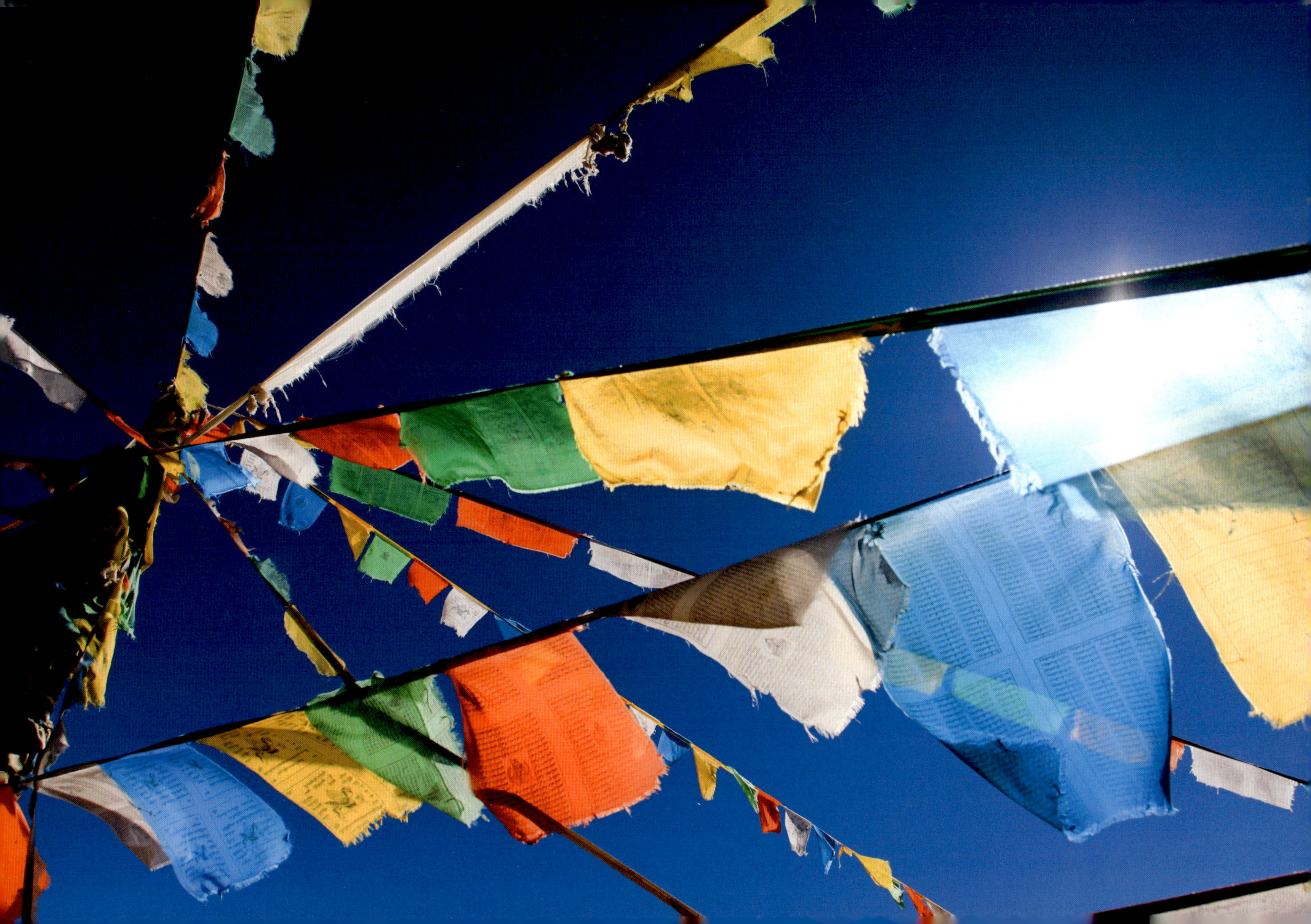

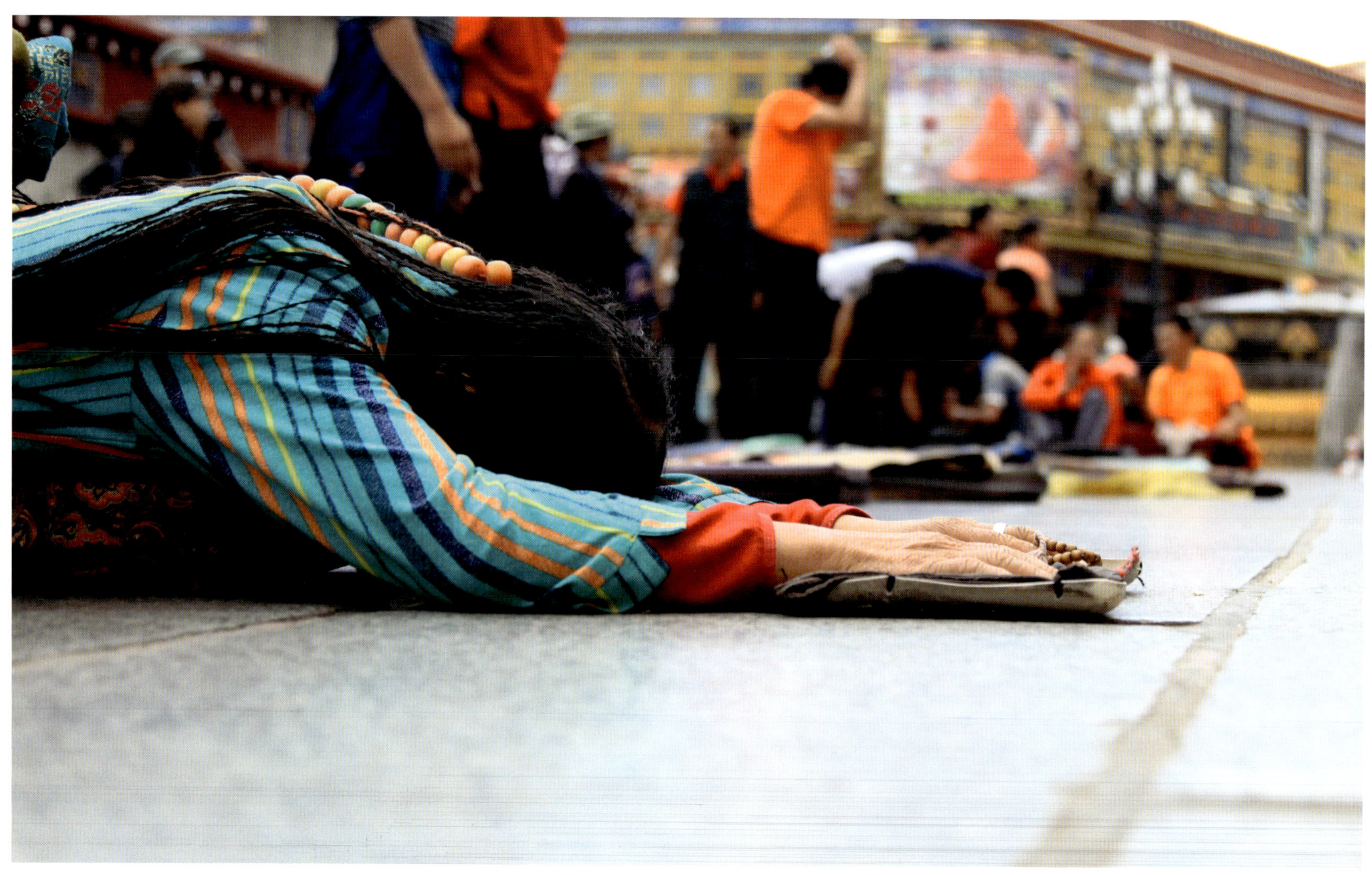

Tibet / Self-dedication

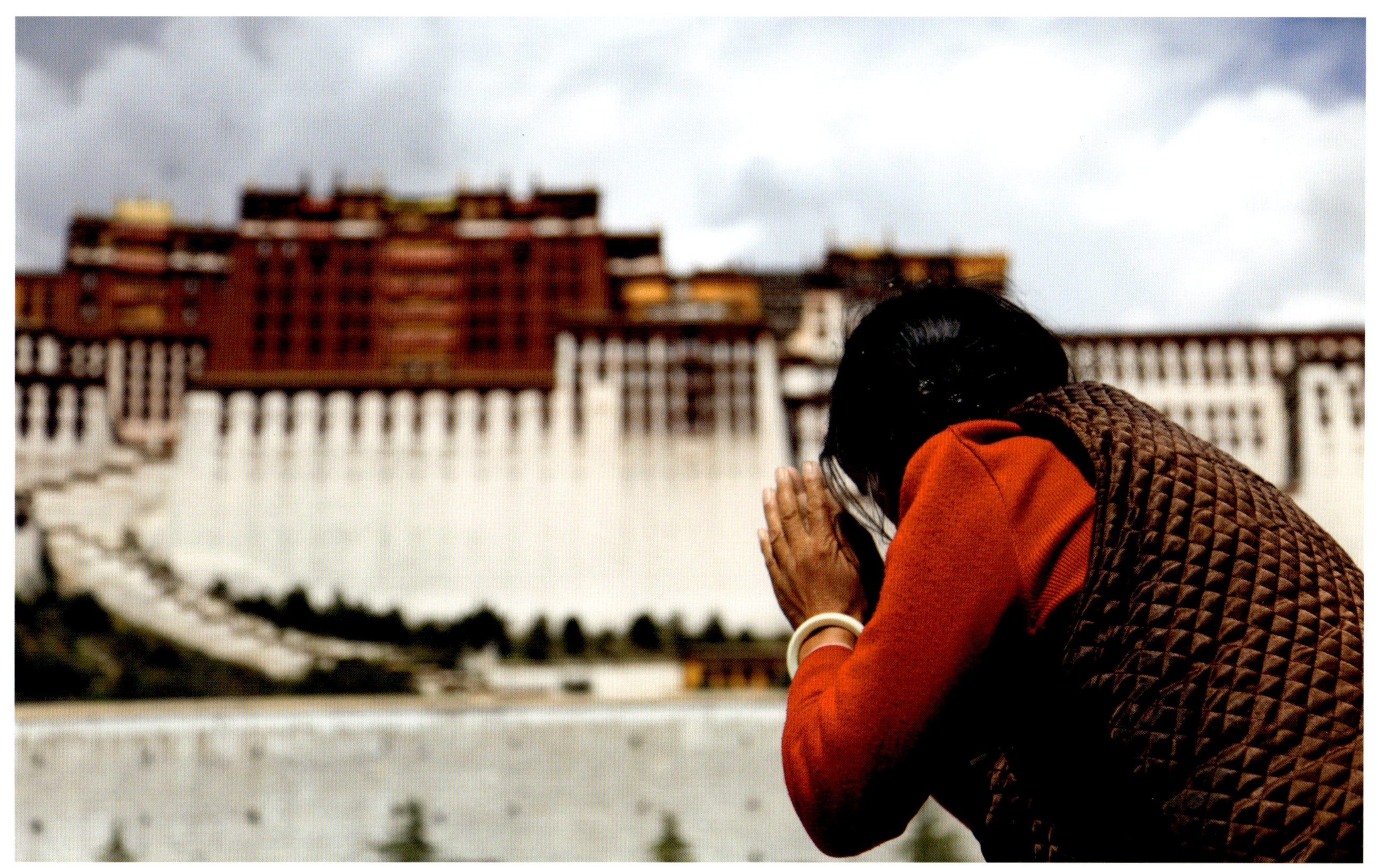

Tibet / Devotions

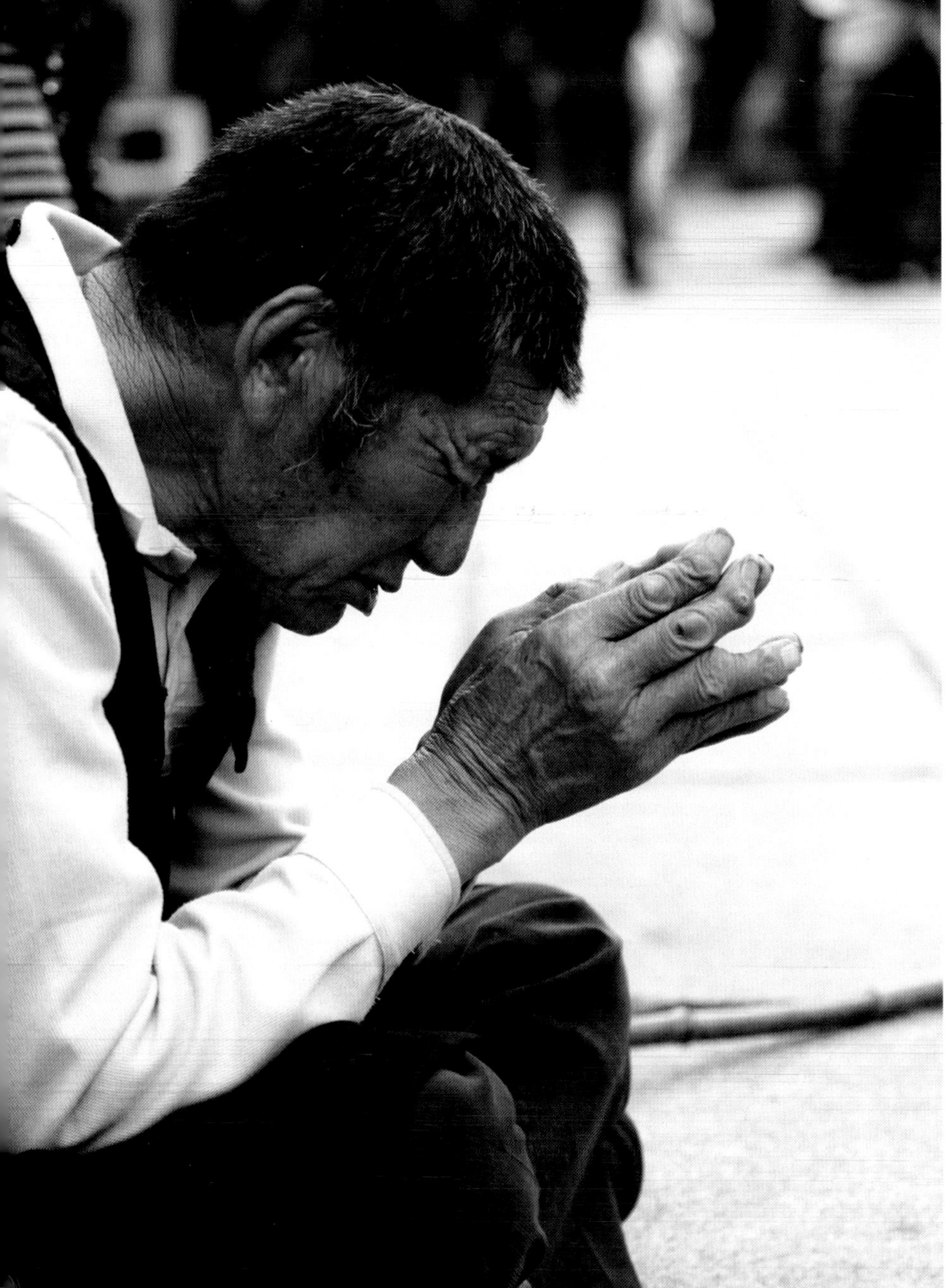

Tibet / Veneration

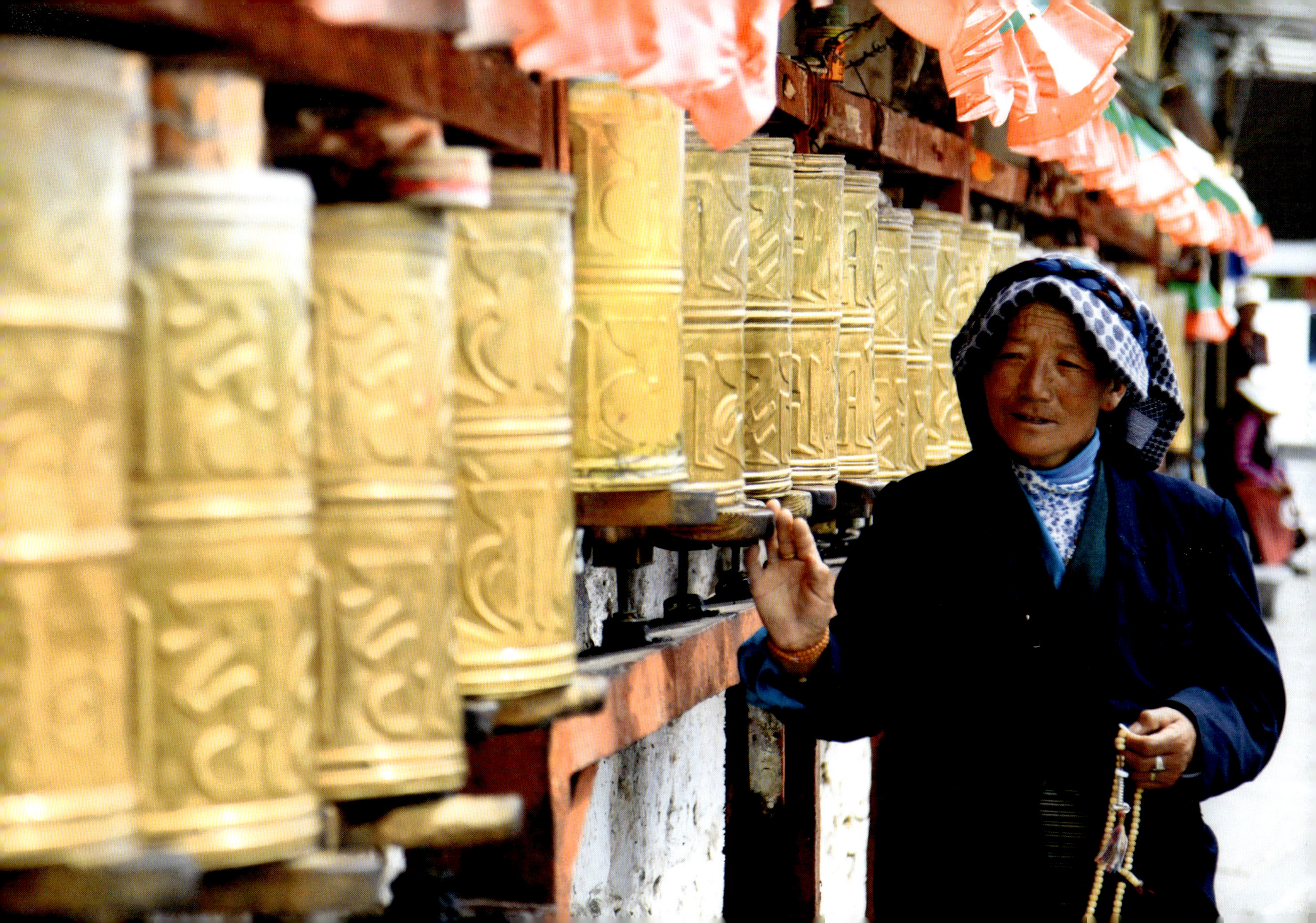

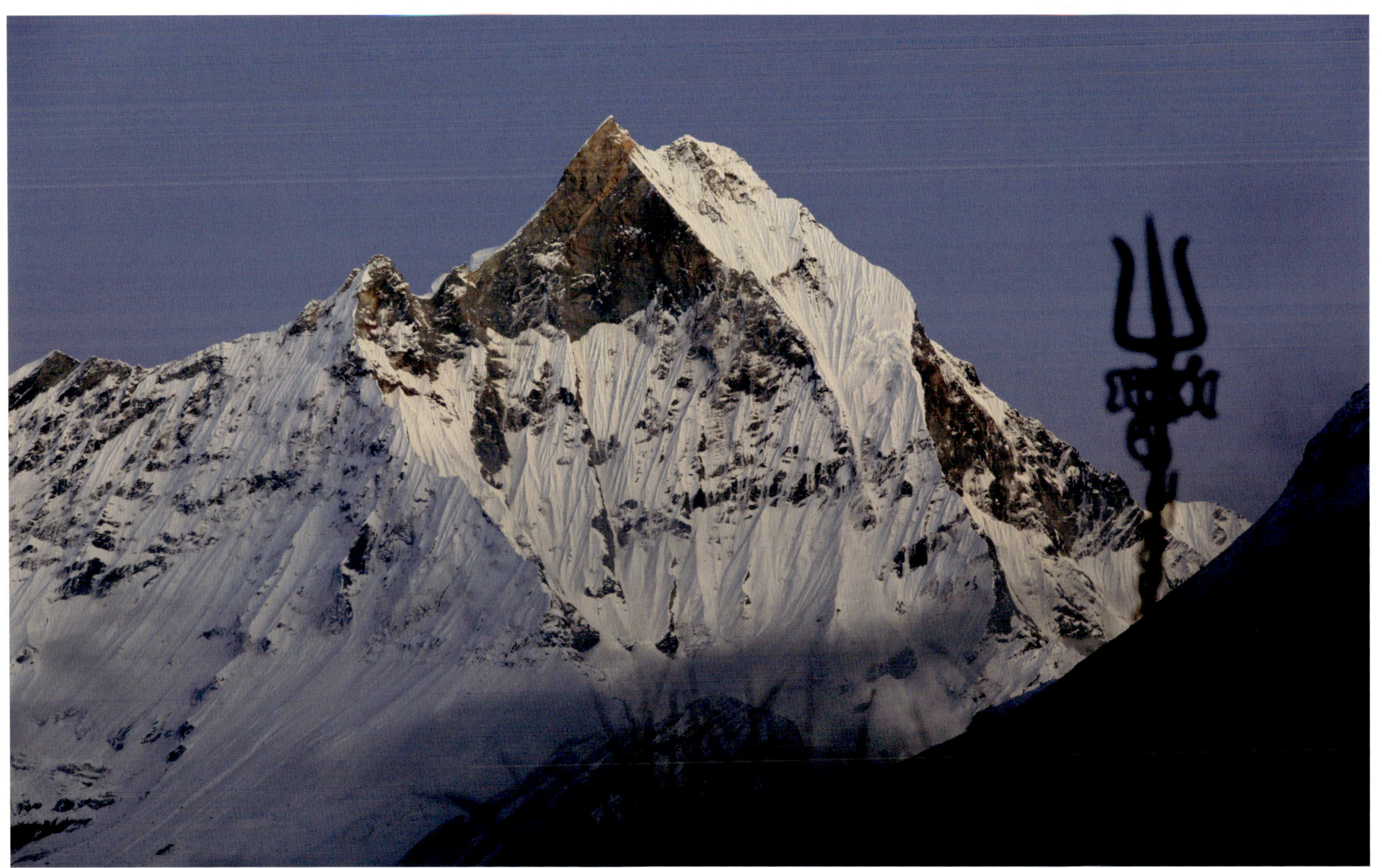

Nepal / Mt.Machapuchare and spear

Nepal / Sunrise of the Buddha

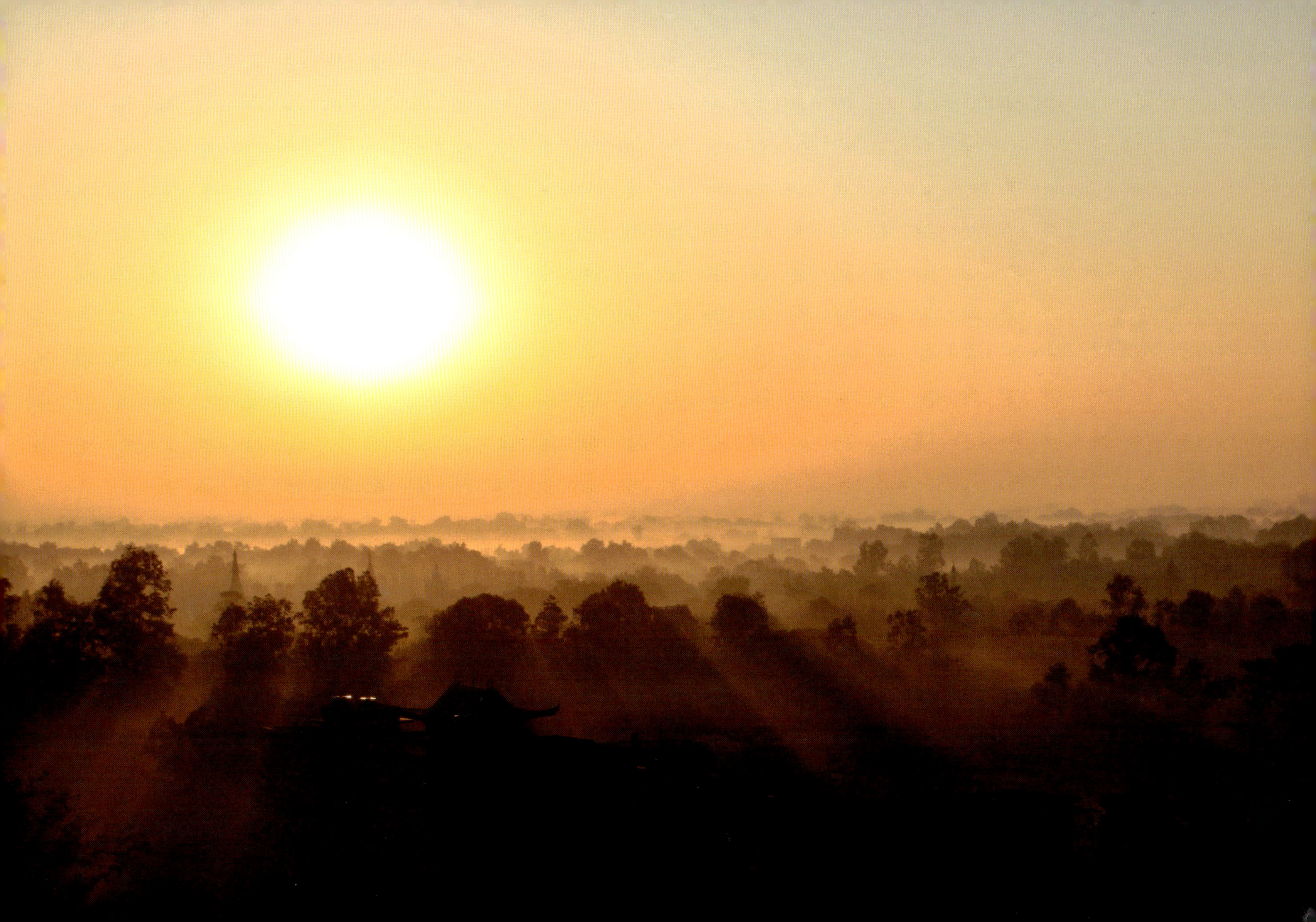

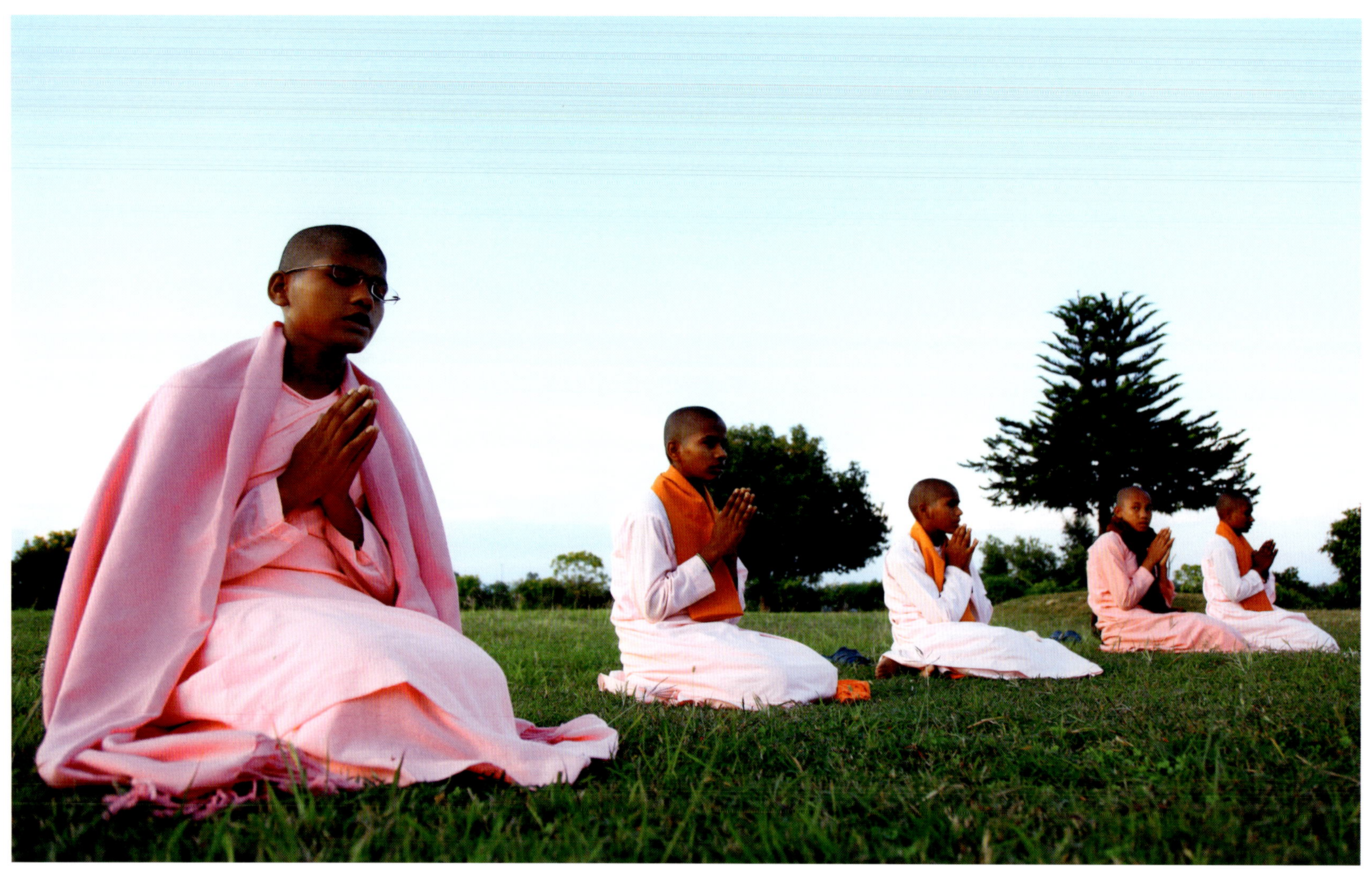

Nepal / Prayer of nuns

10

Nepal / Sunset over Mt.Everest

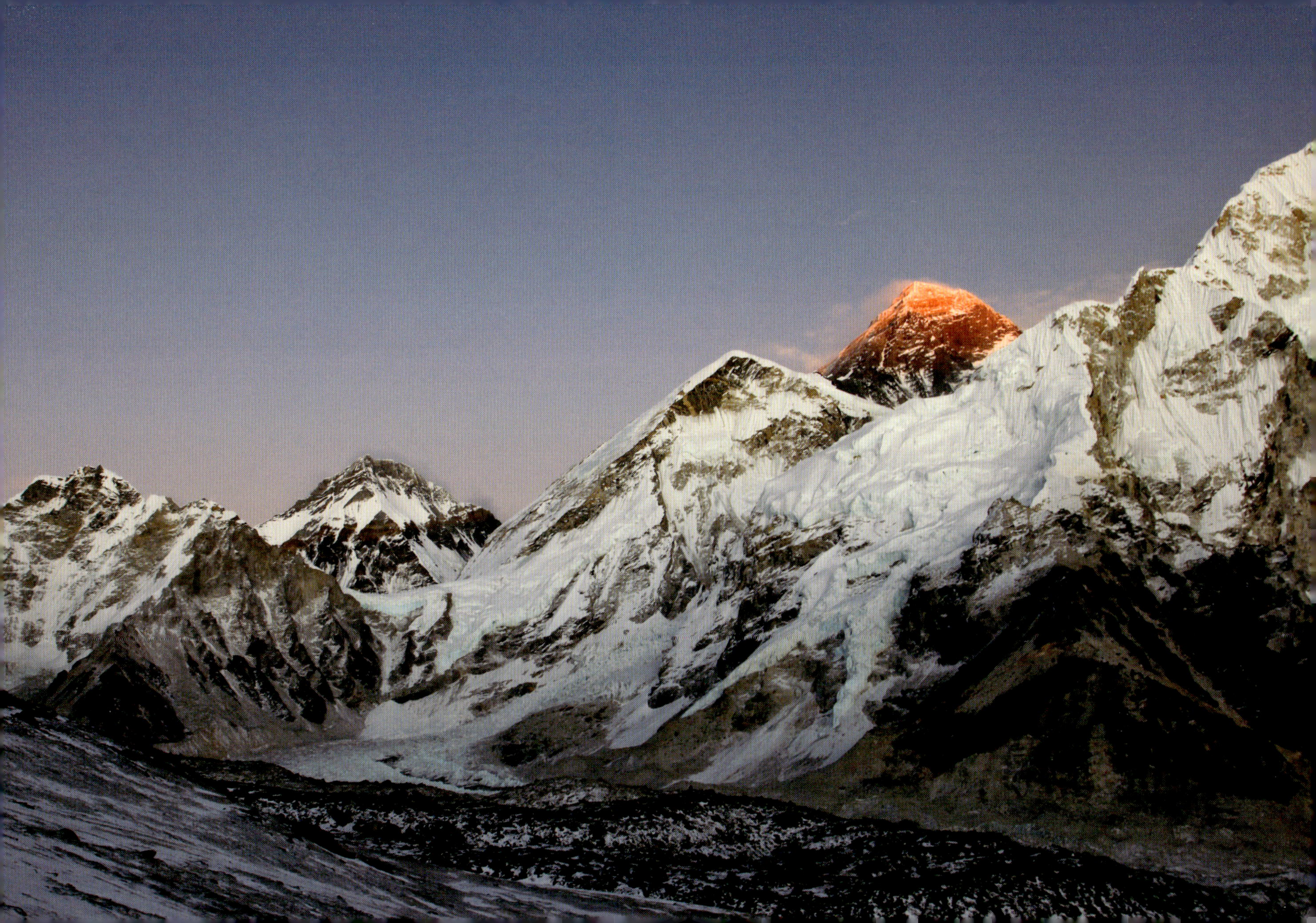

no matter what religion and race

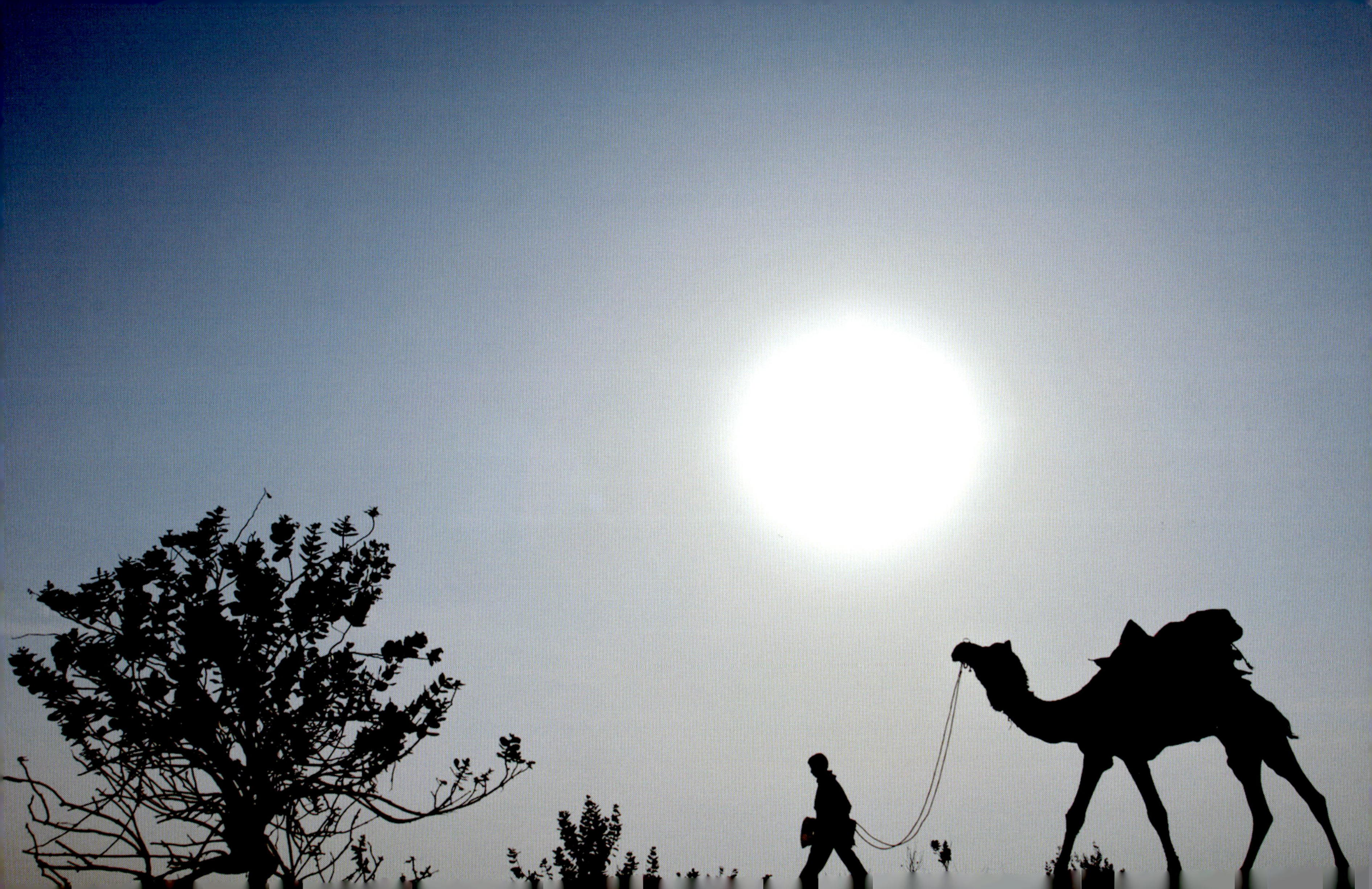

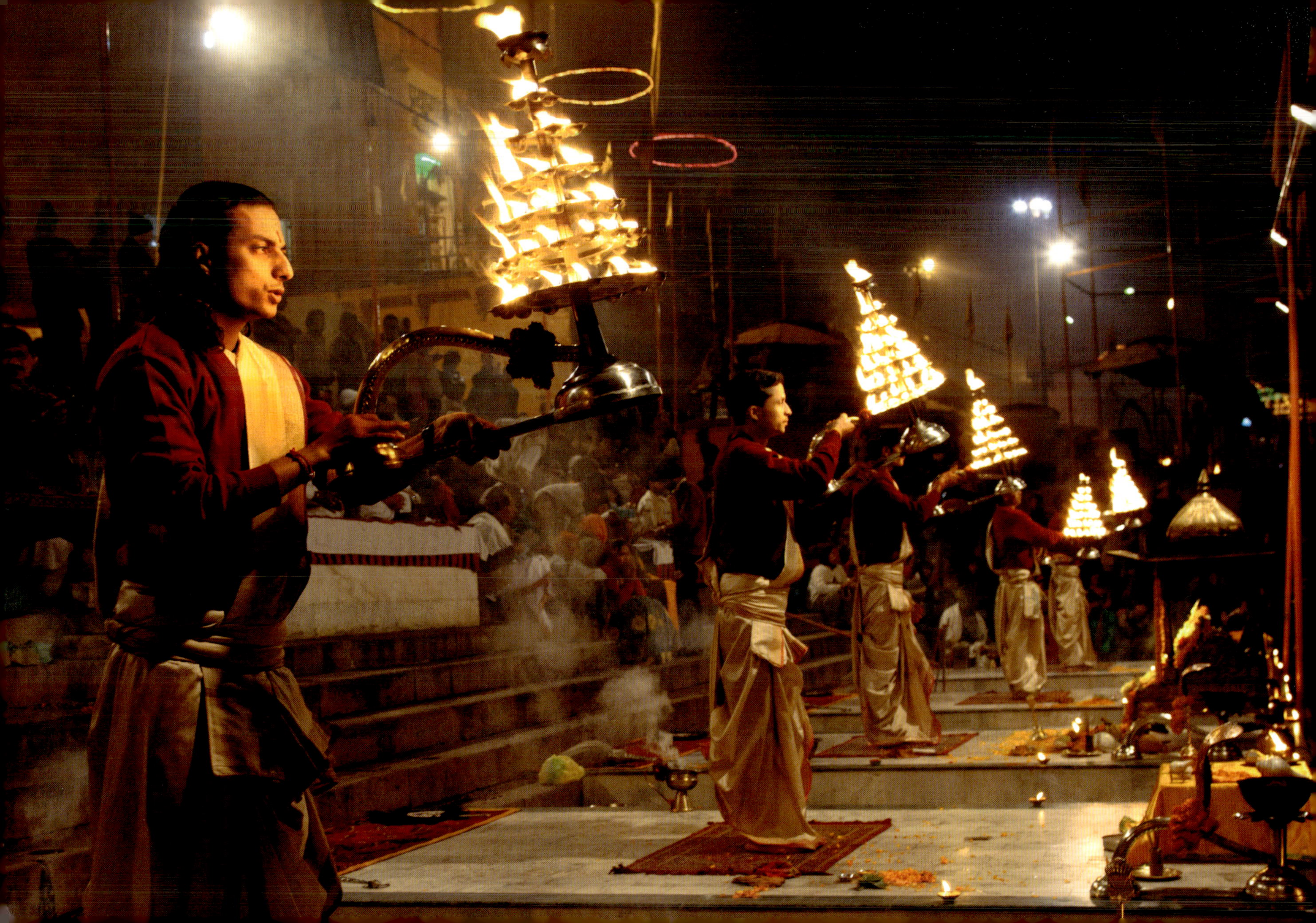

India / Puja in Varanasi

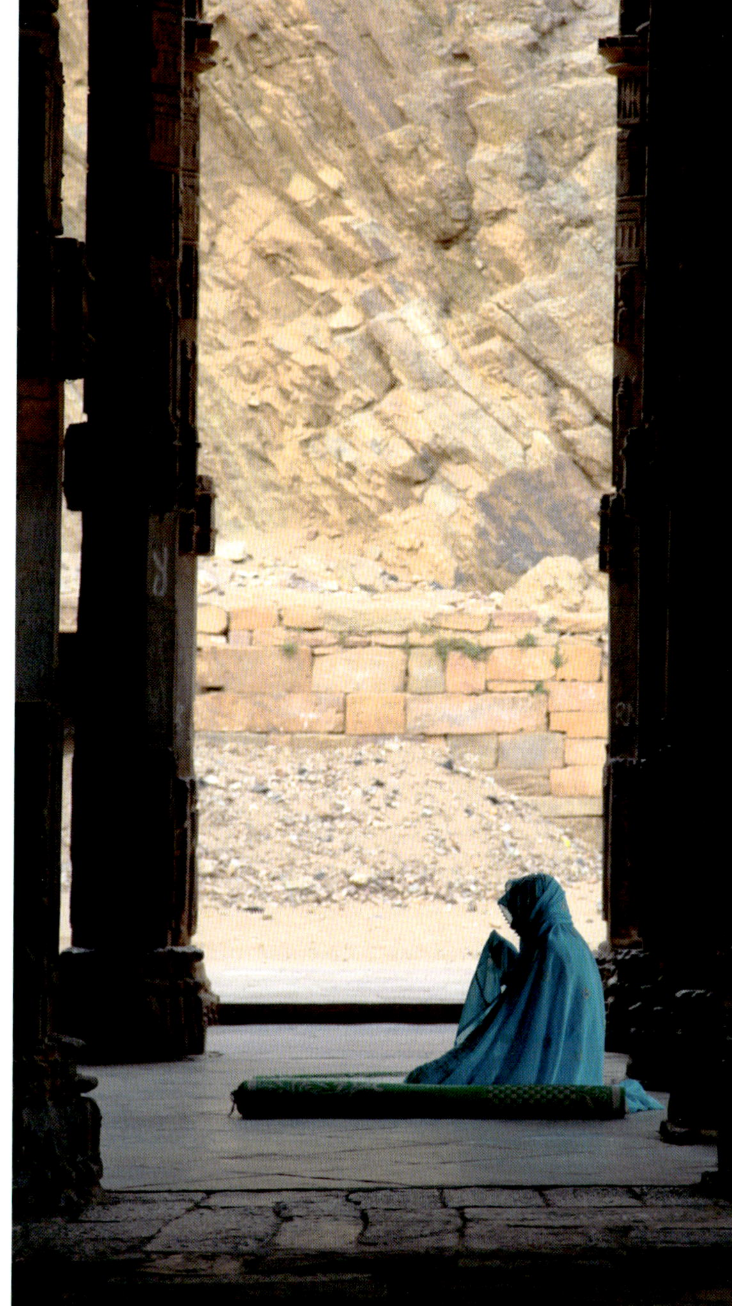

India / Sacred blue

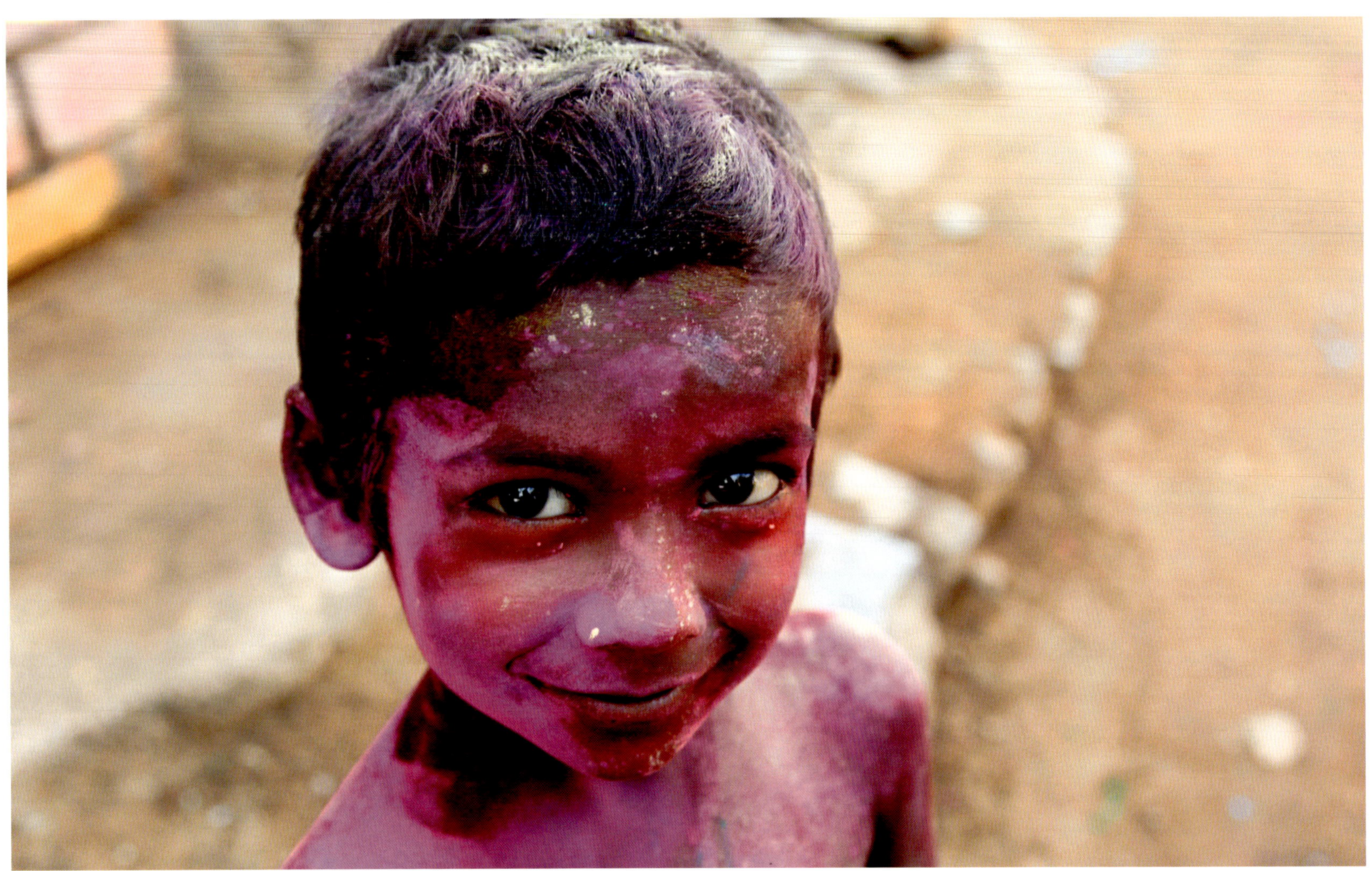

India / Holy boy

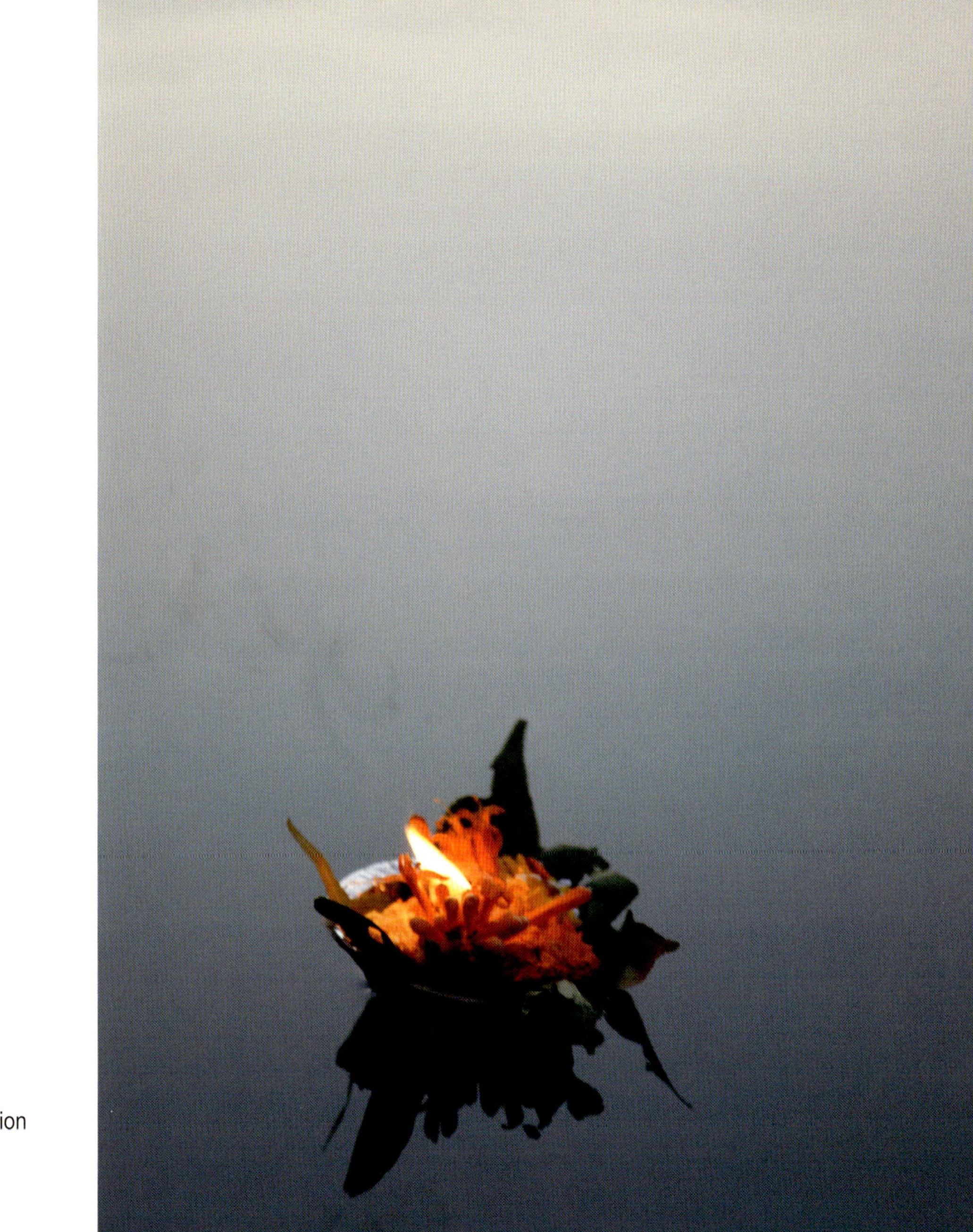

India / The flames of consecration

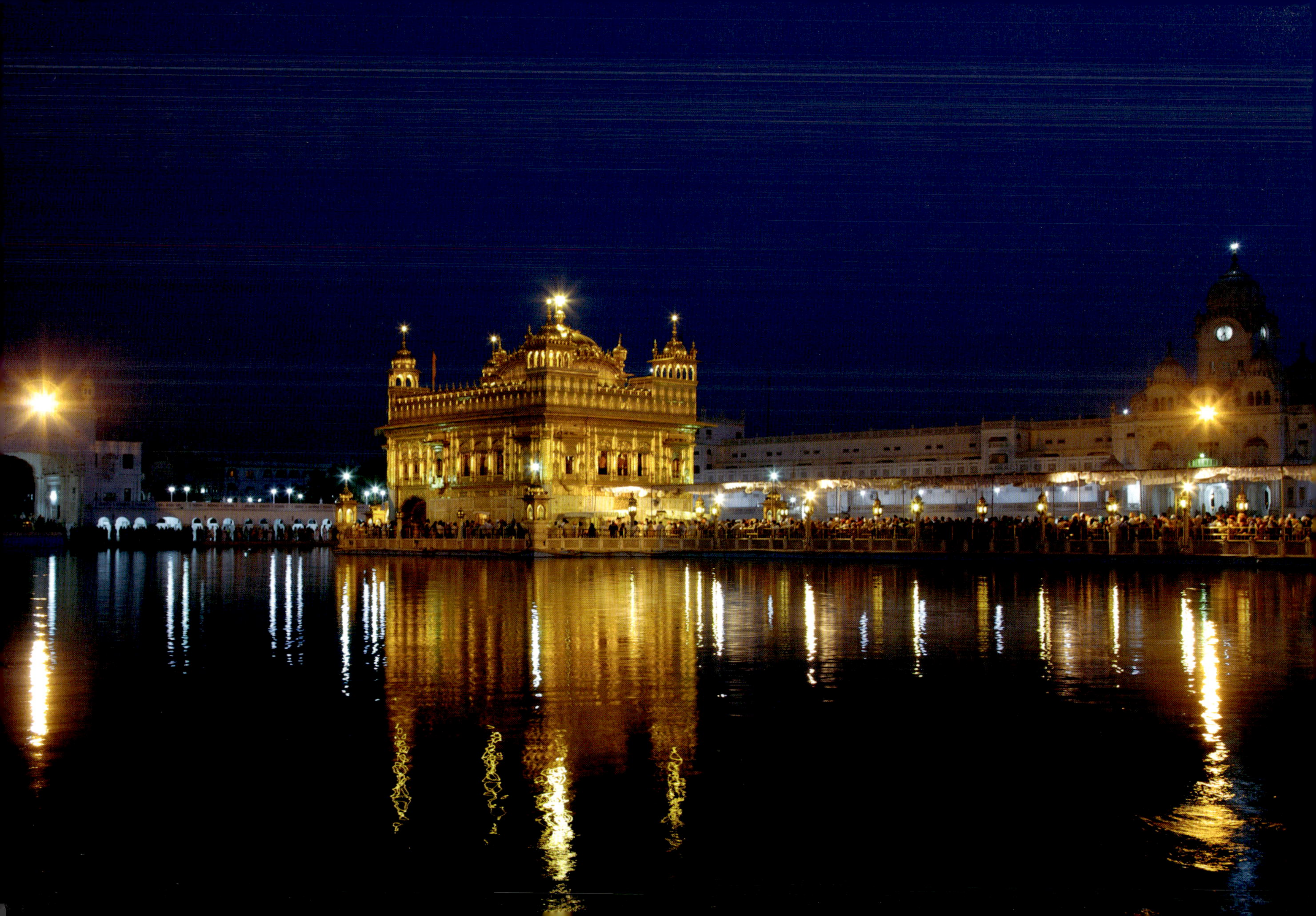

India / Night in the Golden Temple

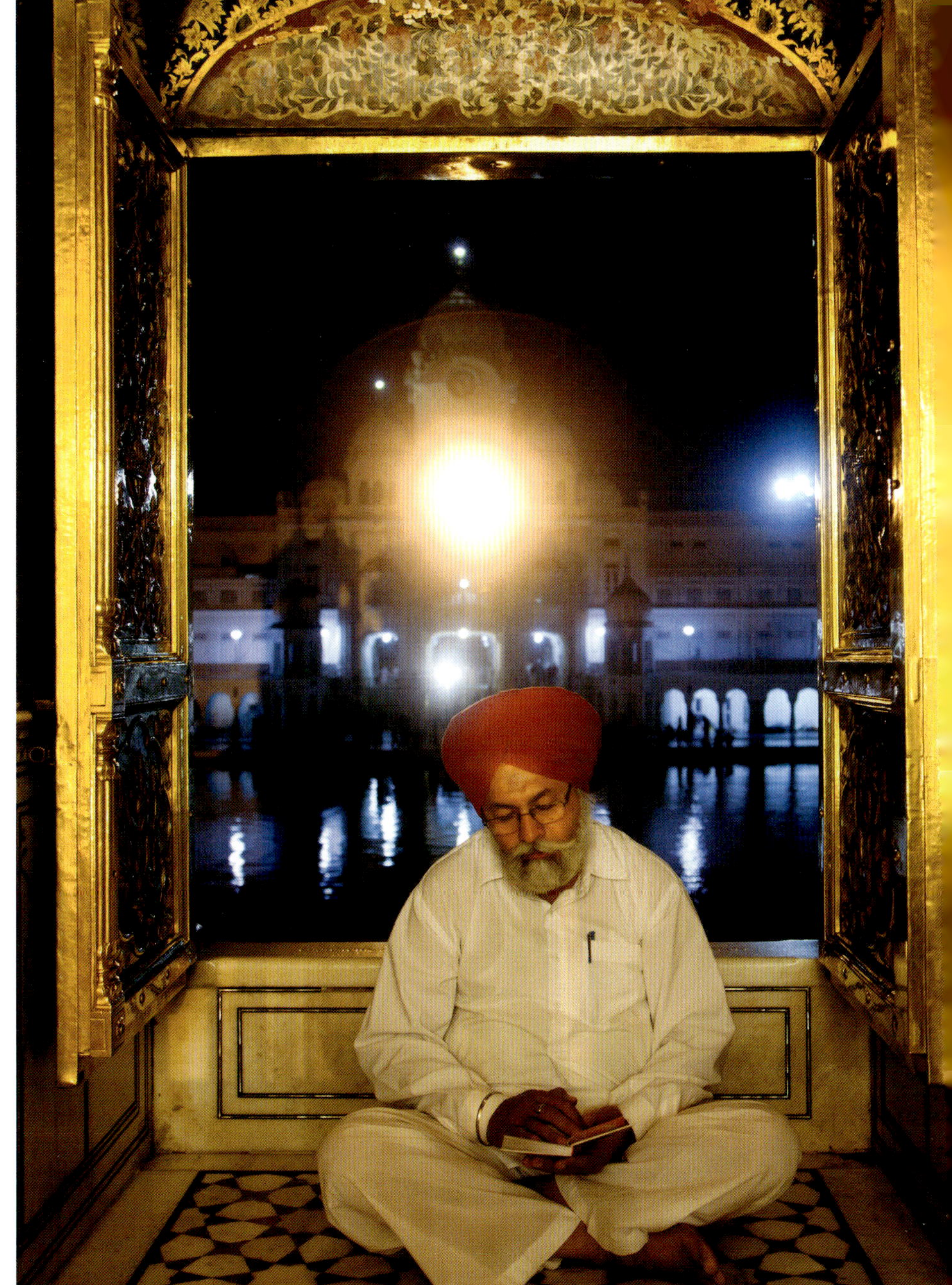

India / Holy time

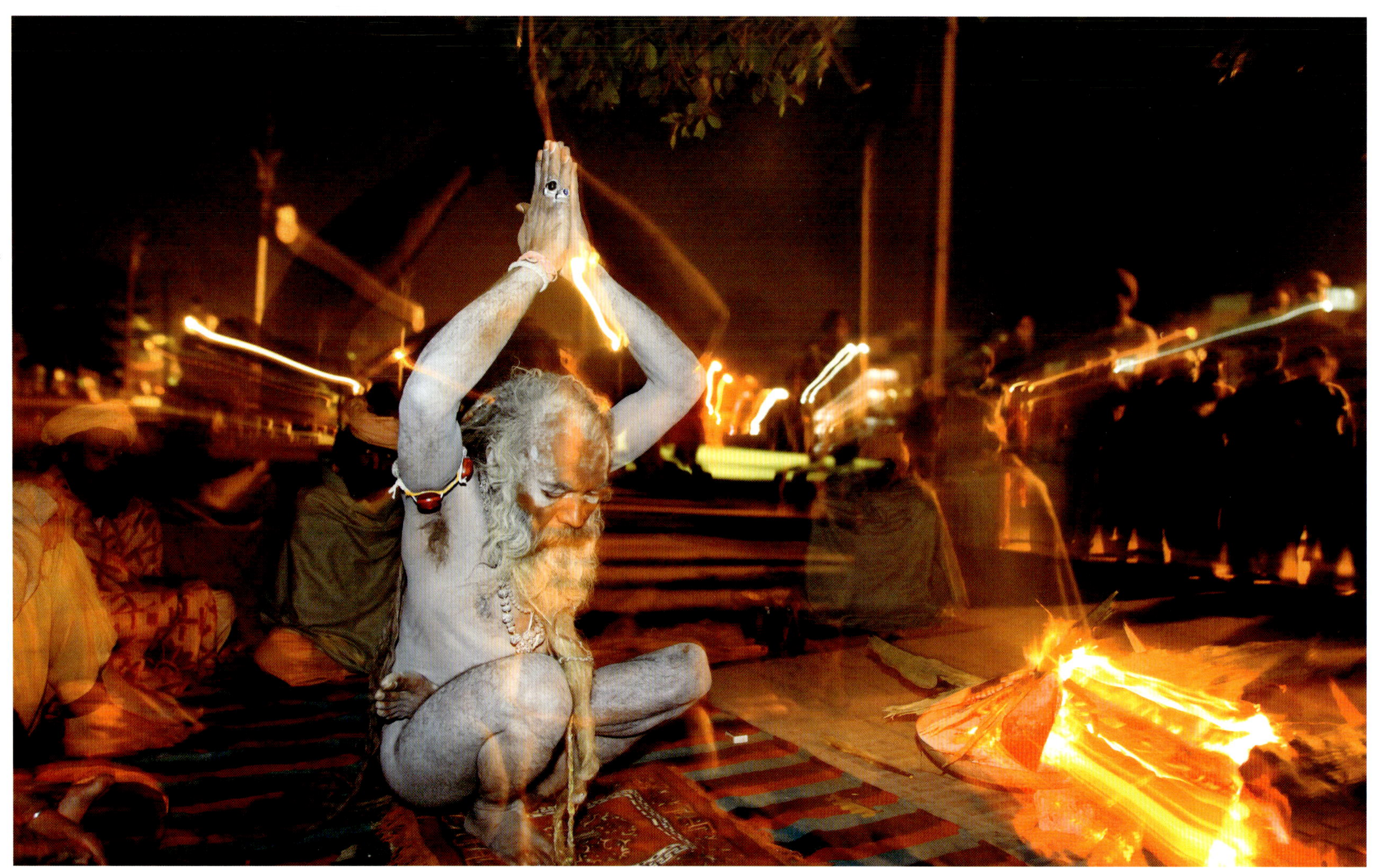

India / Prayer of sadhu

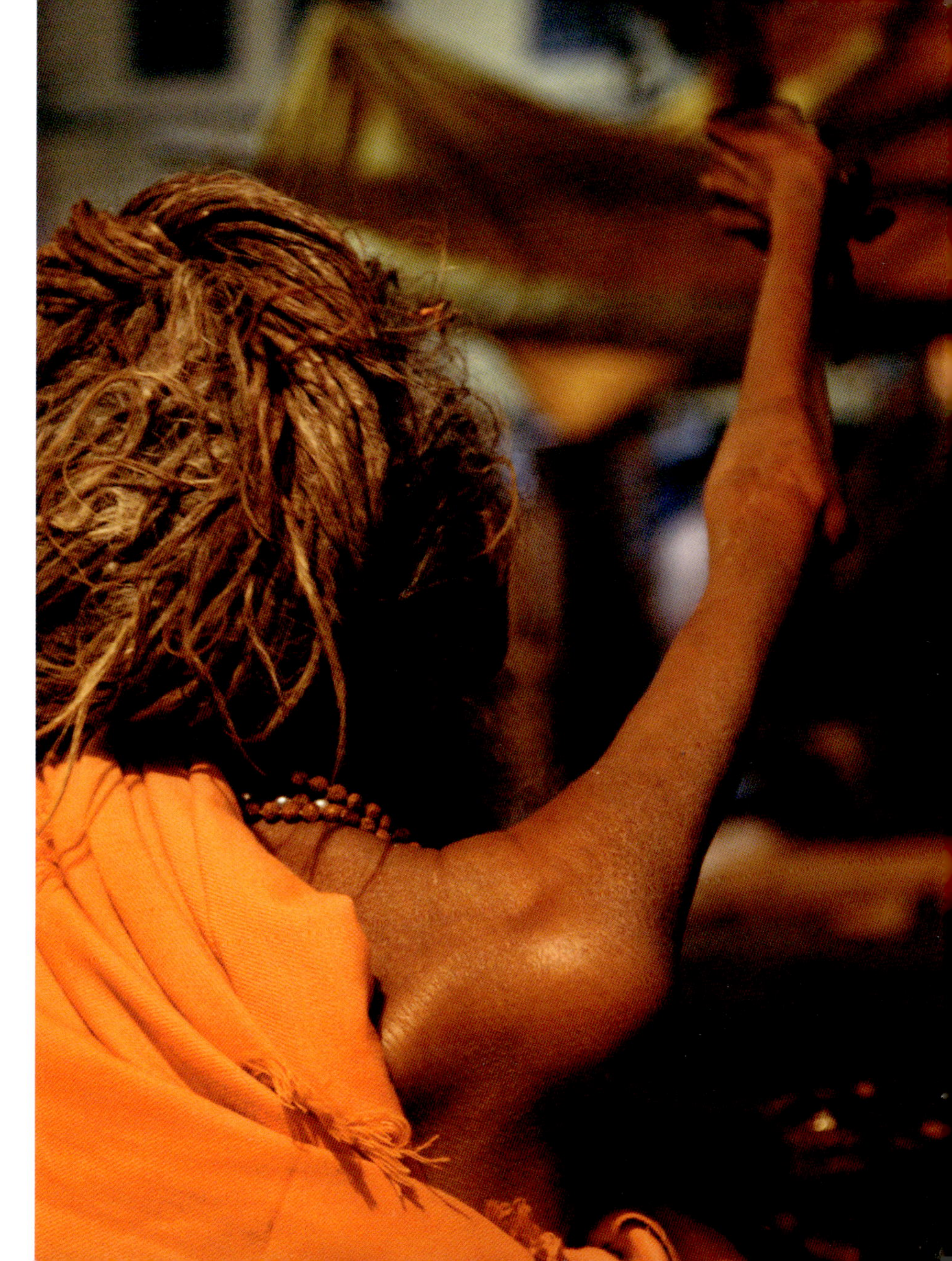

India / Back of ascetic

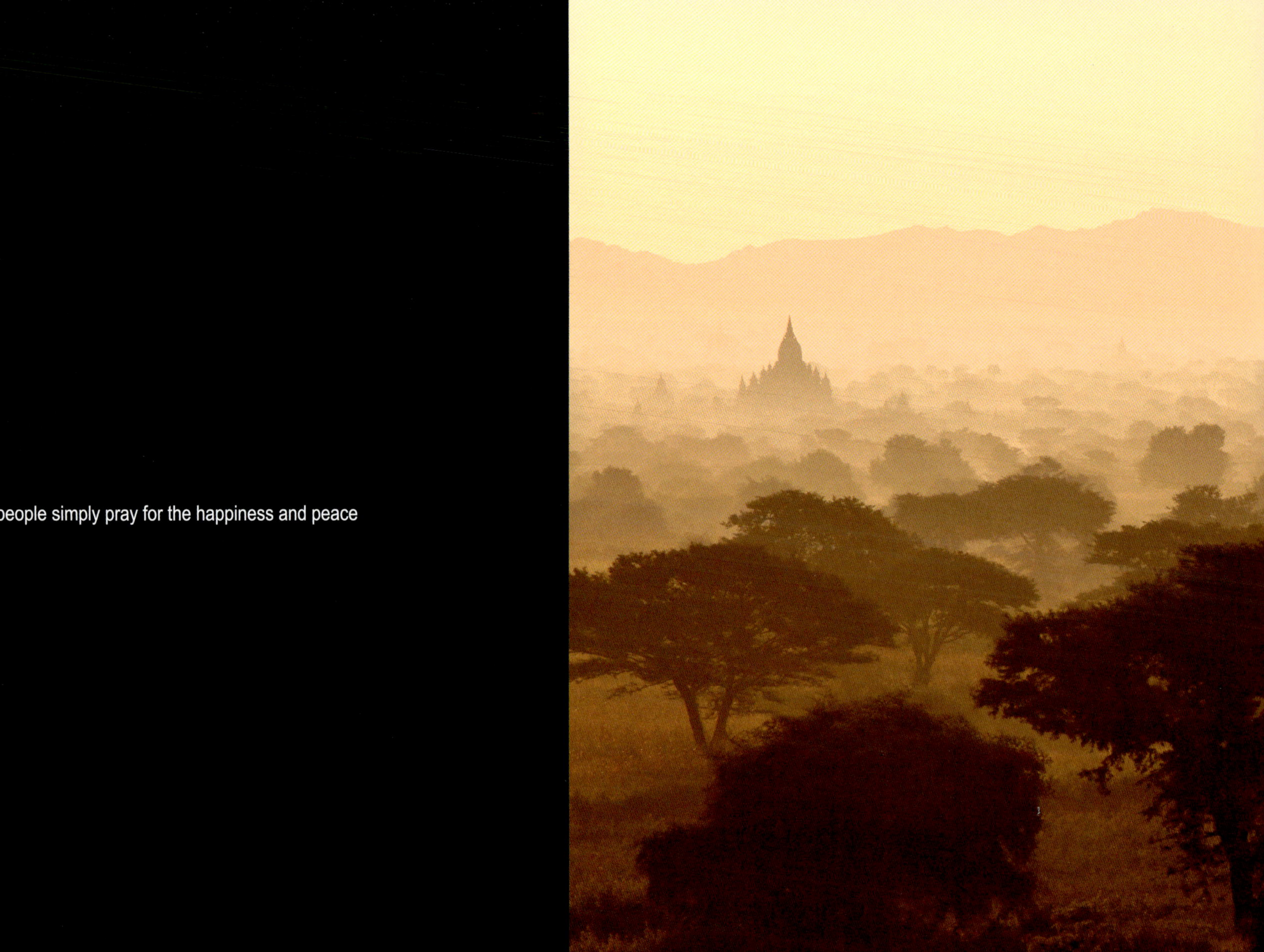
people simply pray for the happiness and peace

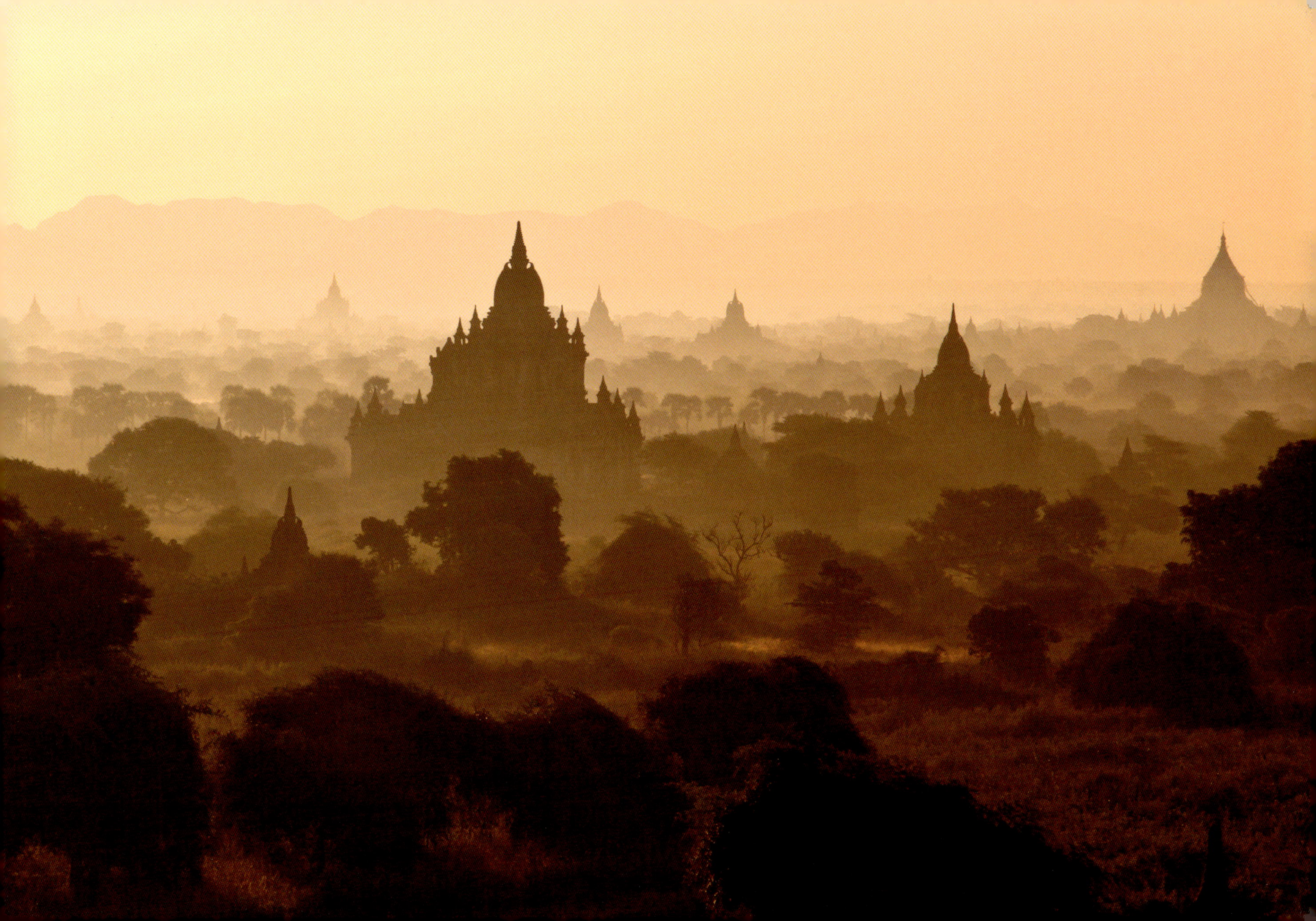

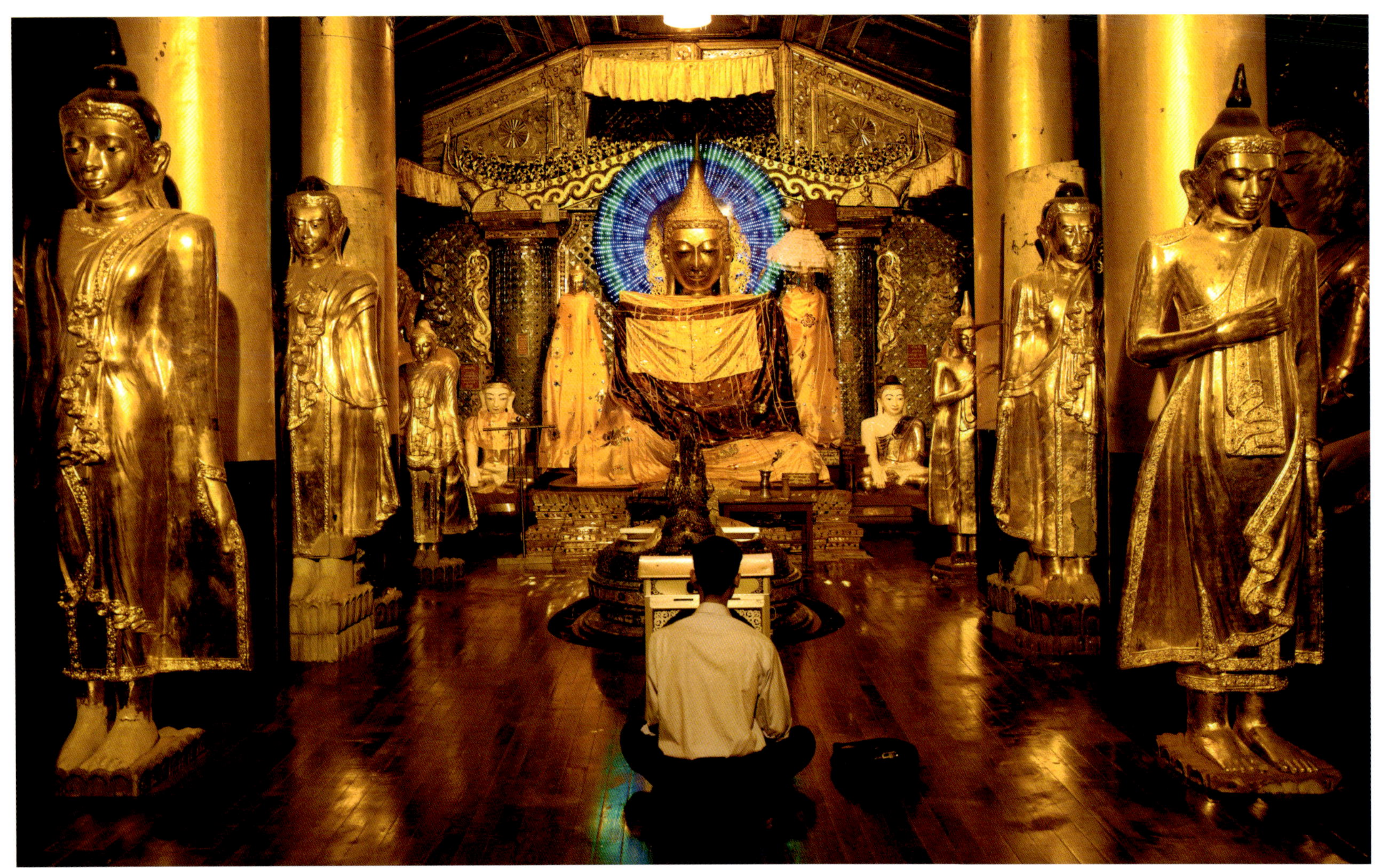

Burma / Sacred precincts

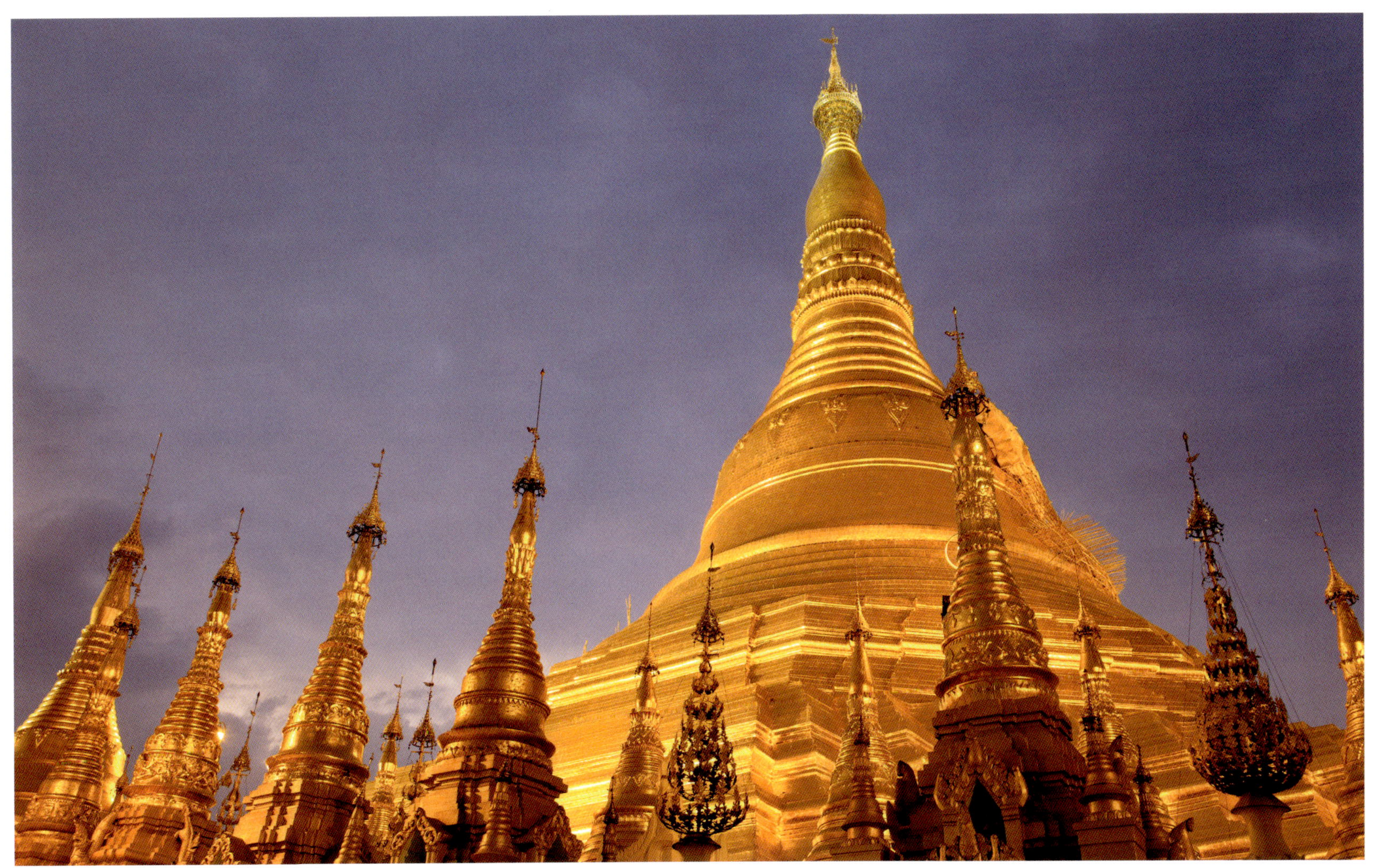

Burma / Shwedagon Pagoda at night

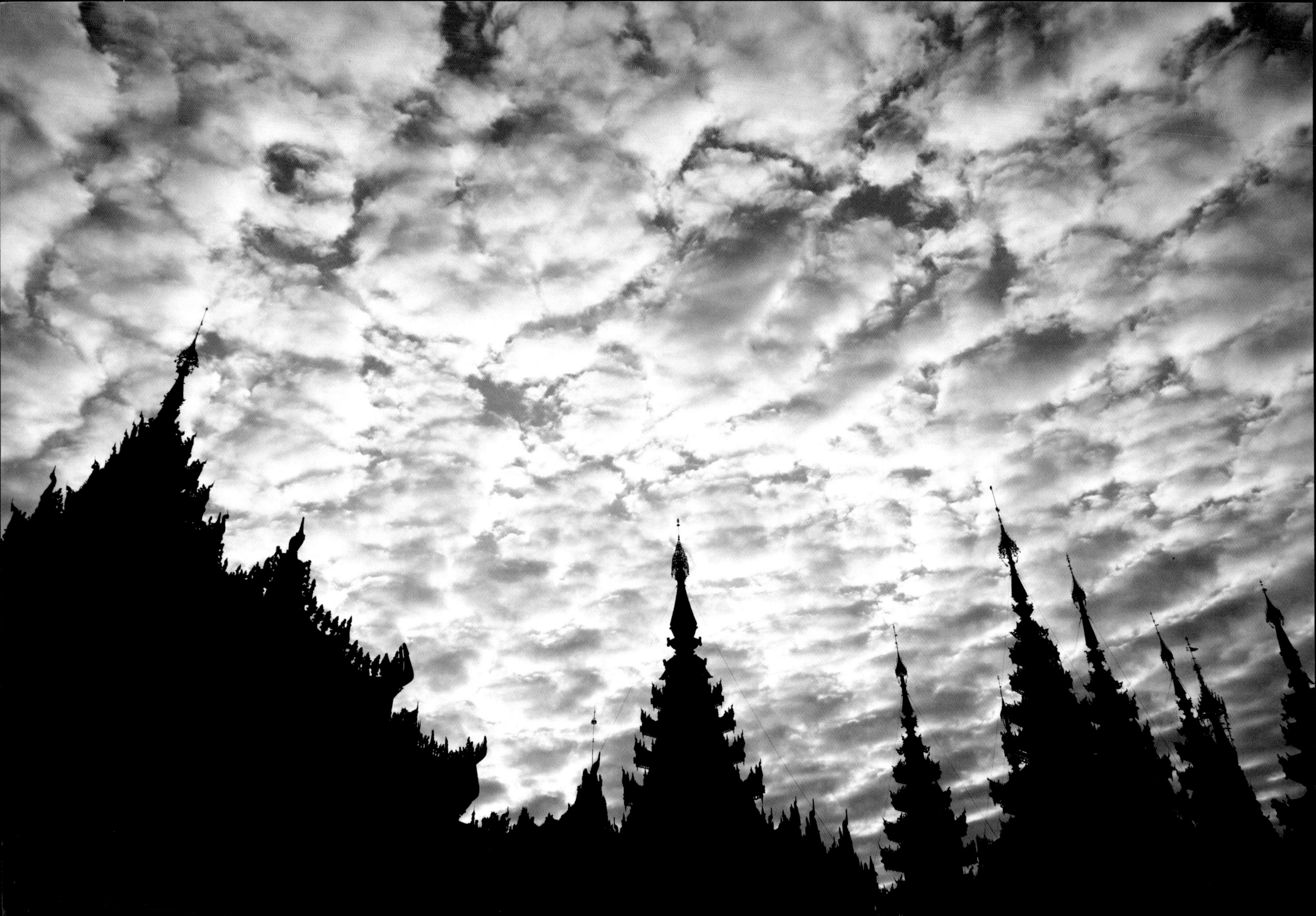

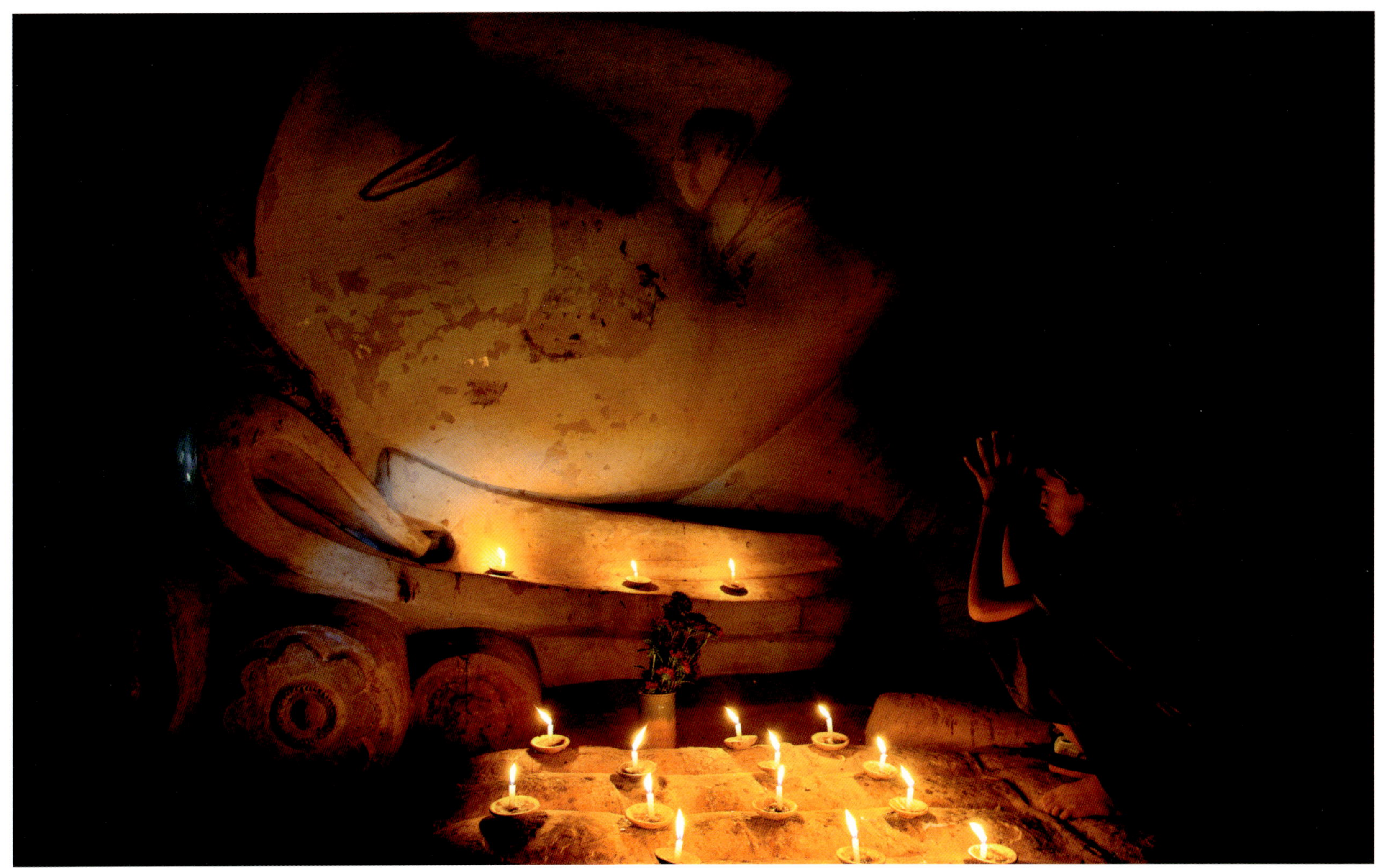

Burma / Boy and reclining Buddha

Burma / Cirrocumulus clouds and Pagoda

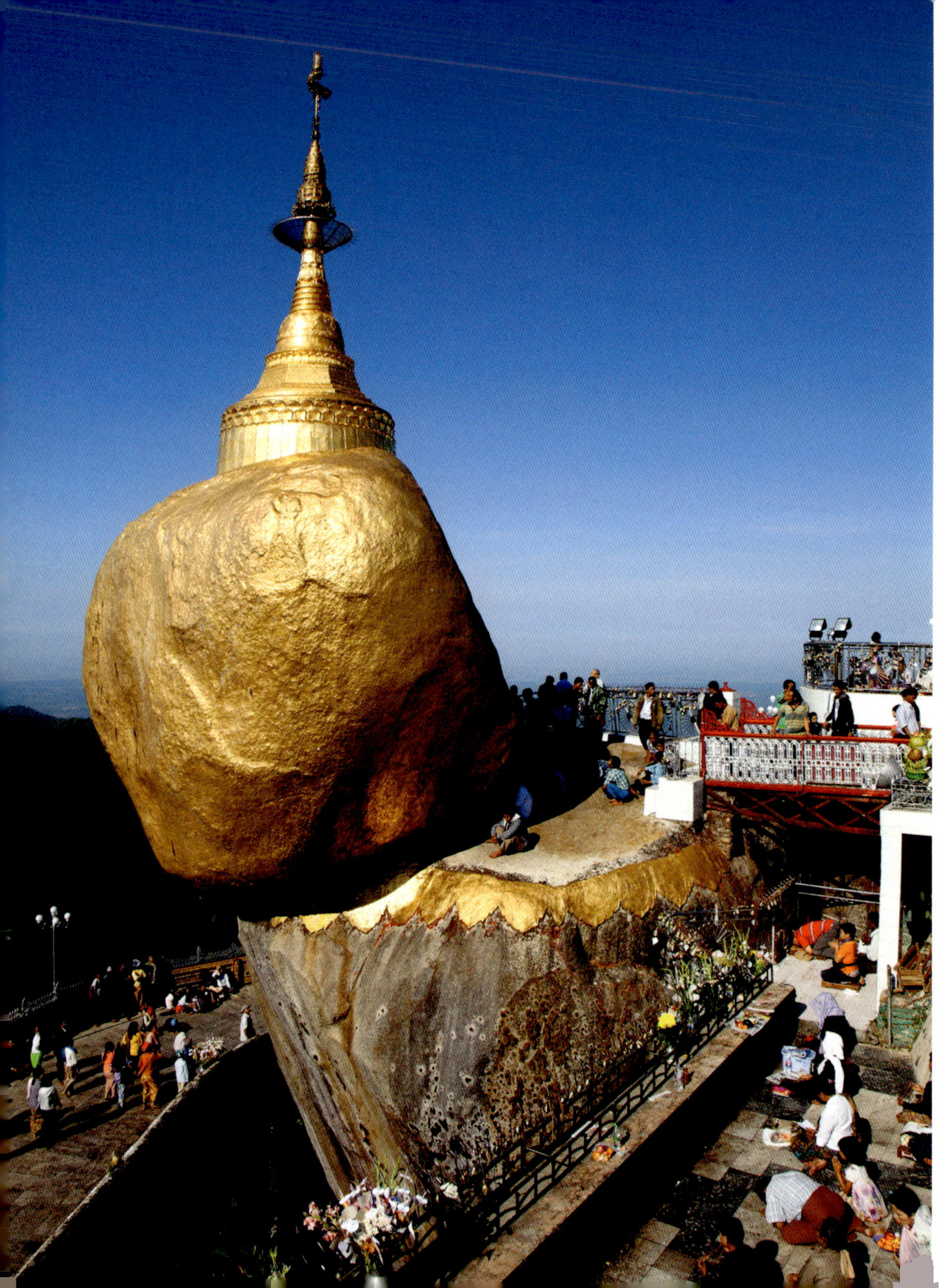

Burma / Golden rock pagoda and blue sky

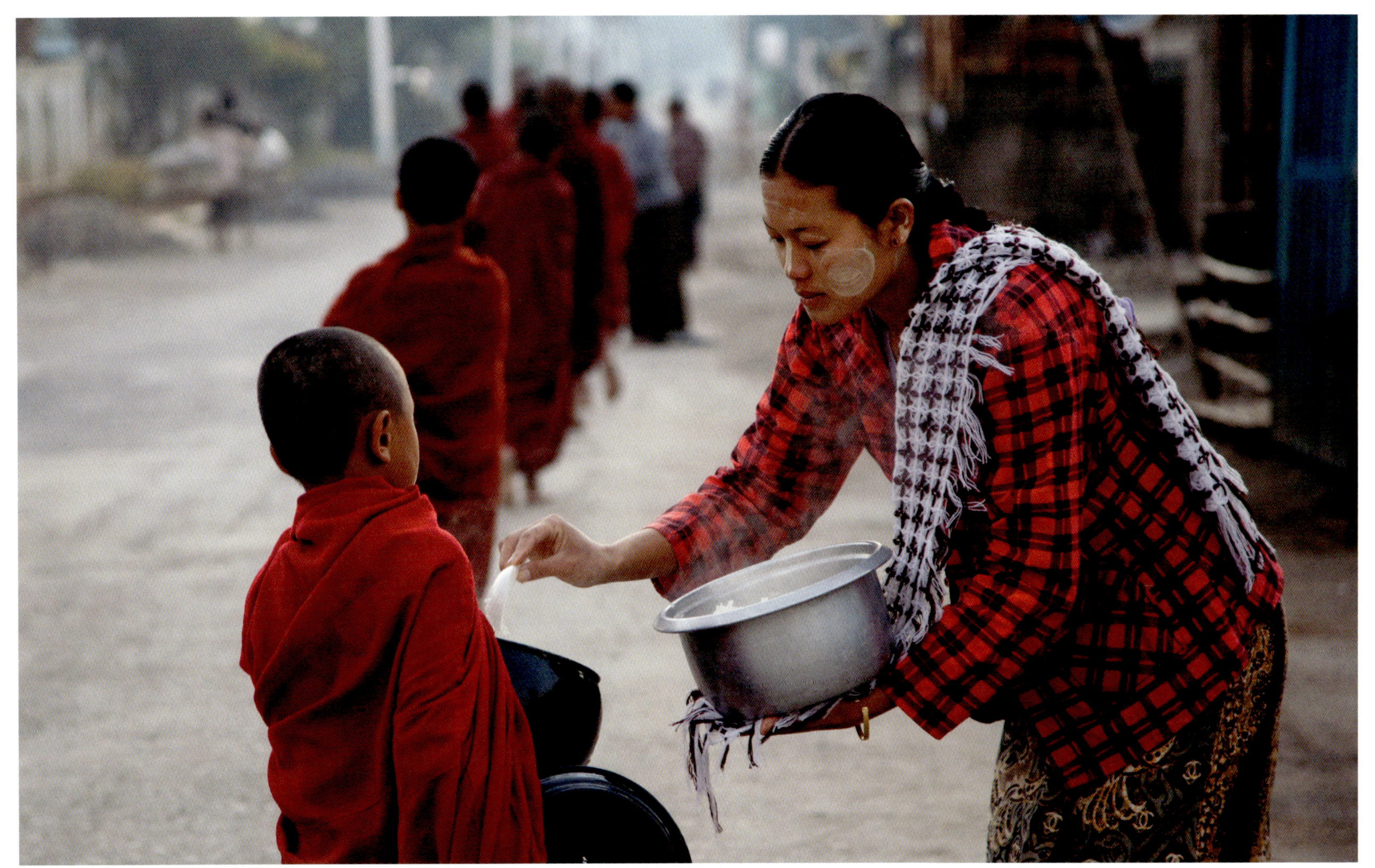

Burma / Mendicant priests

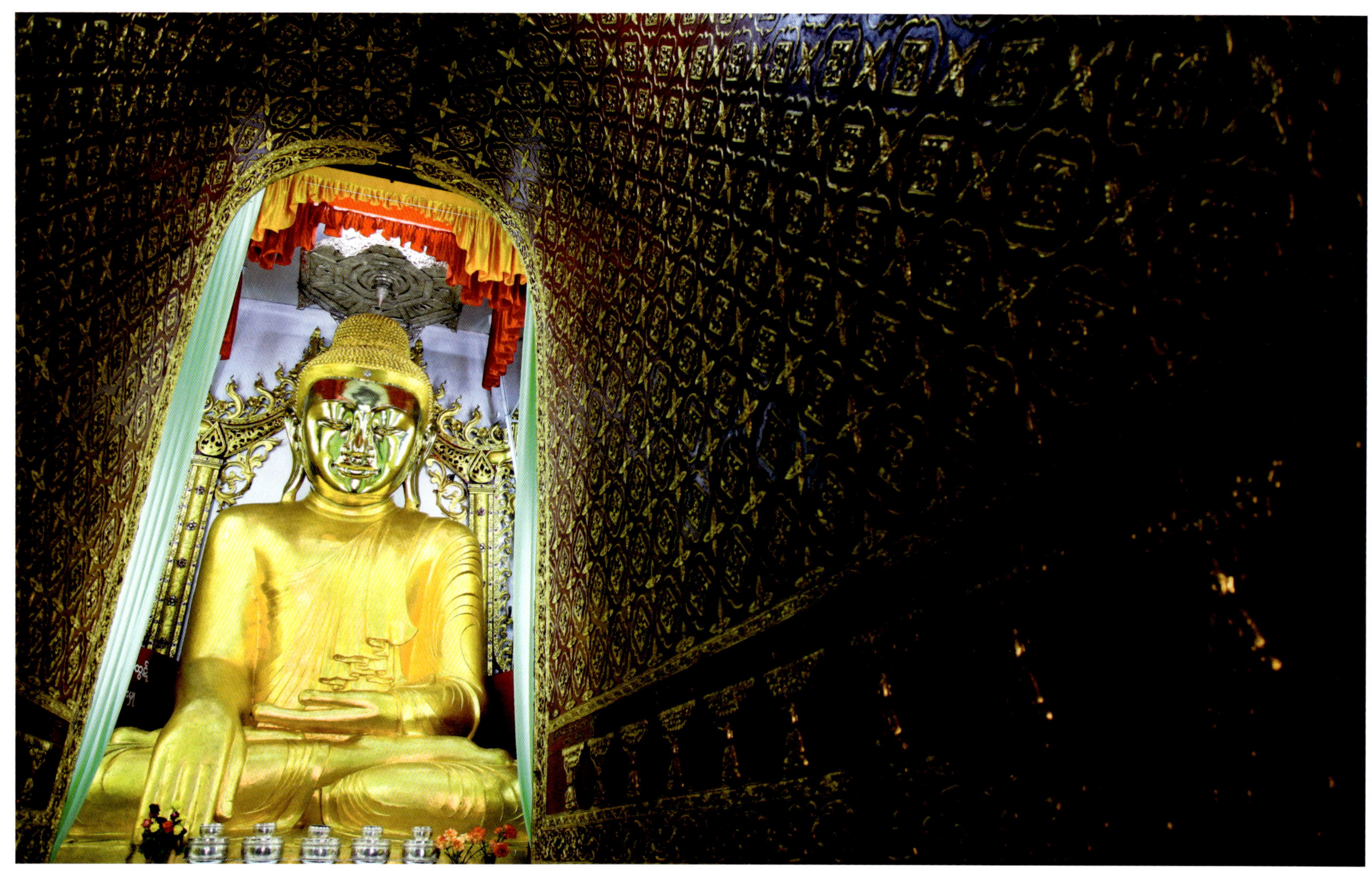

Burma / Radiance of Buddha

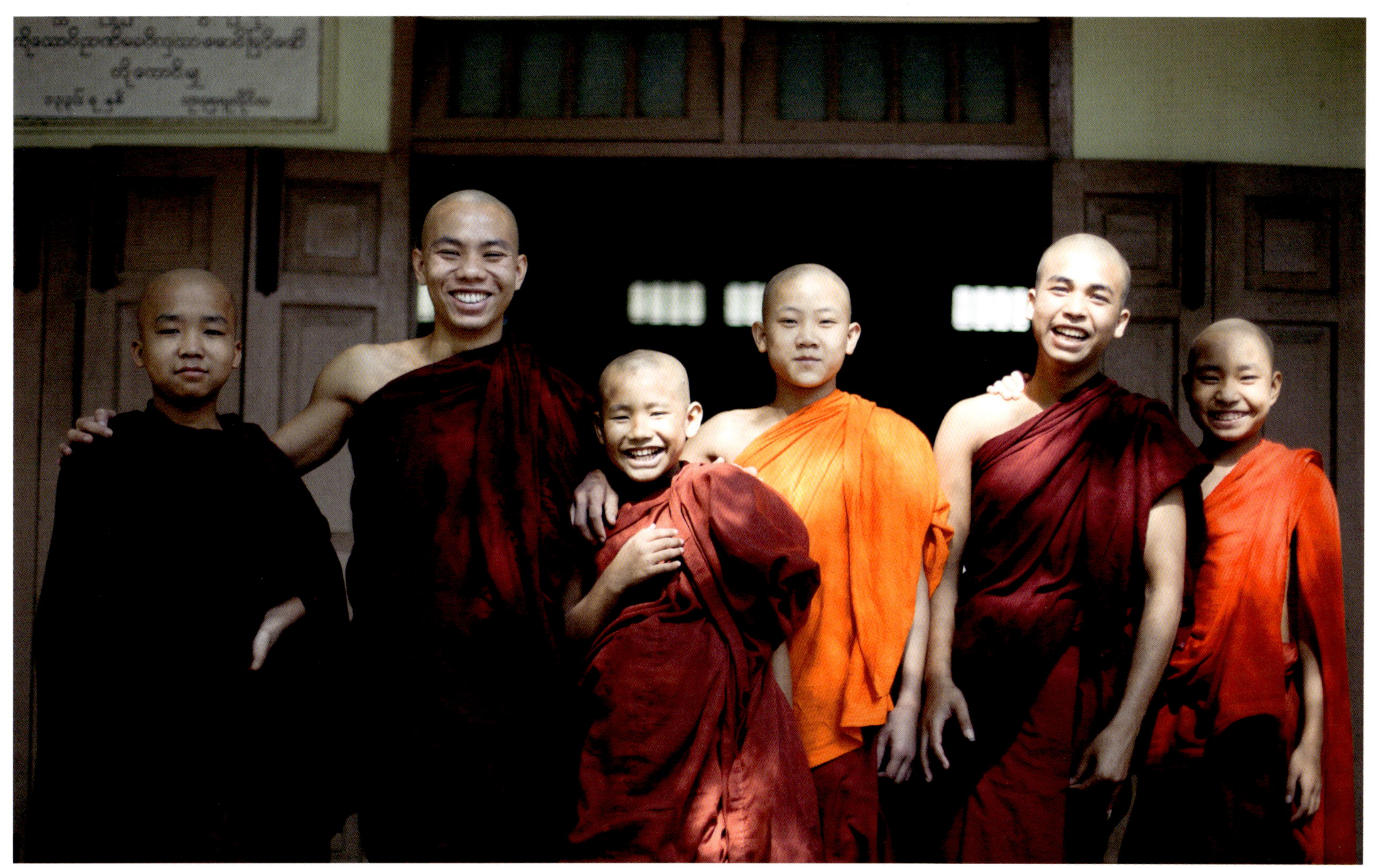

Burma / Smiling monks

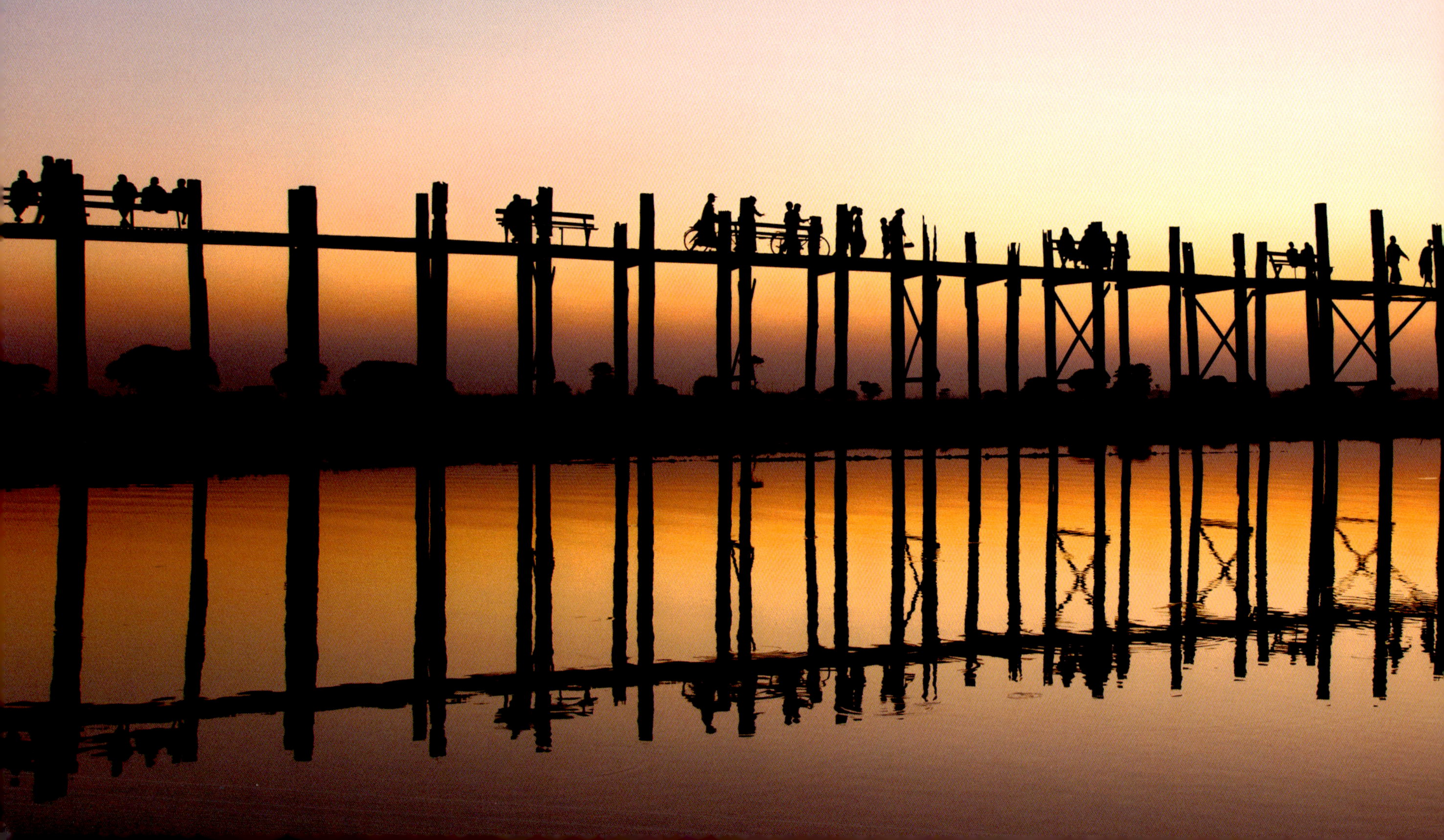

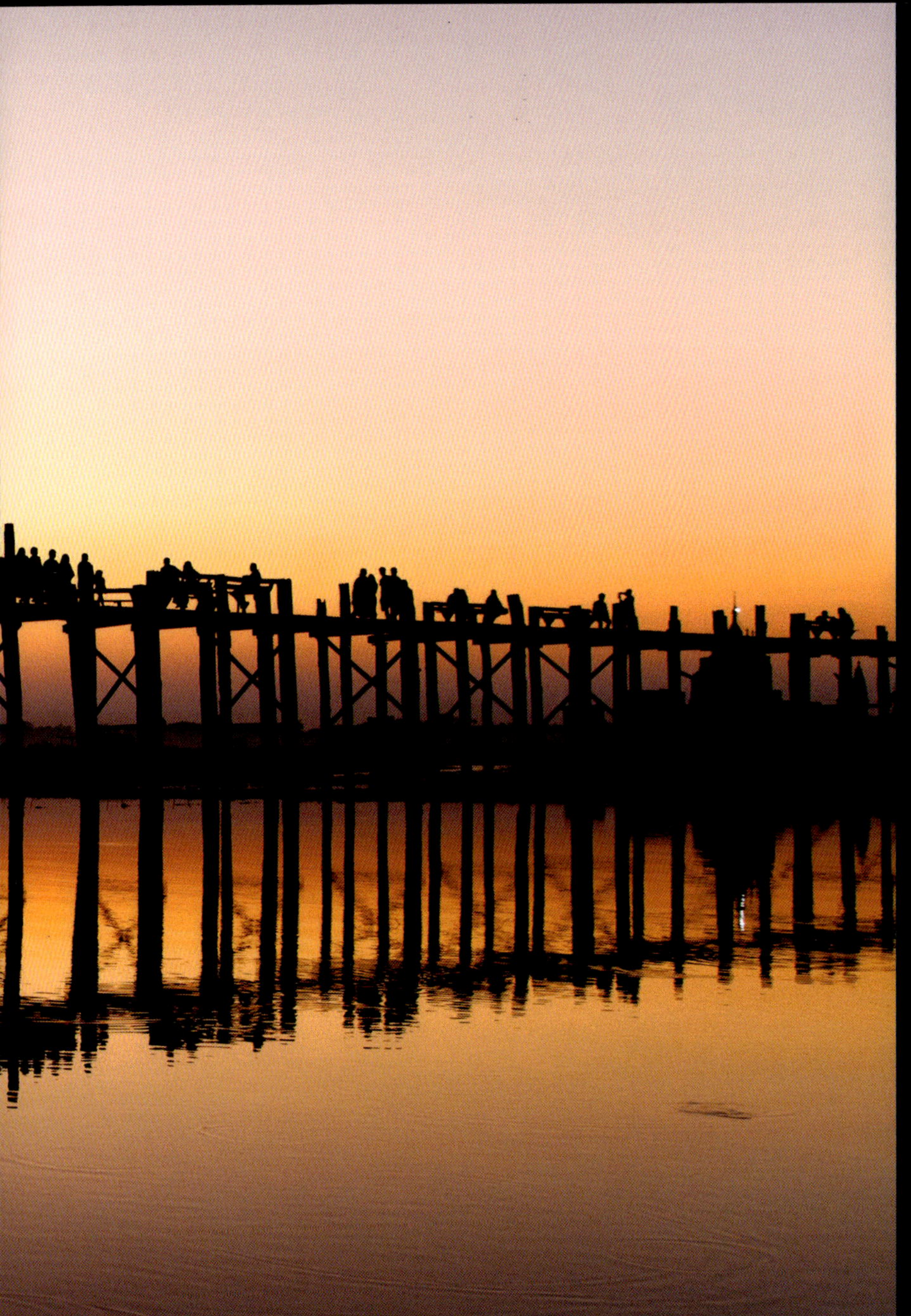

nobody in the world wants foolish war and fight

Burma / Magic hour in Amarapura

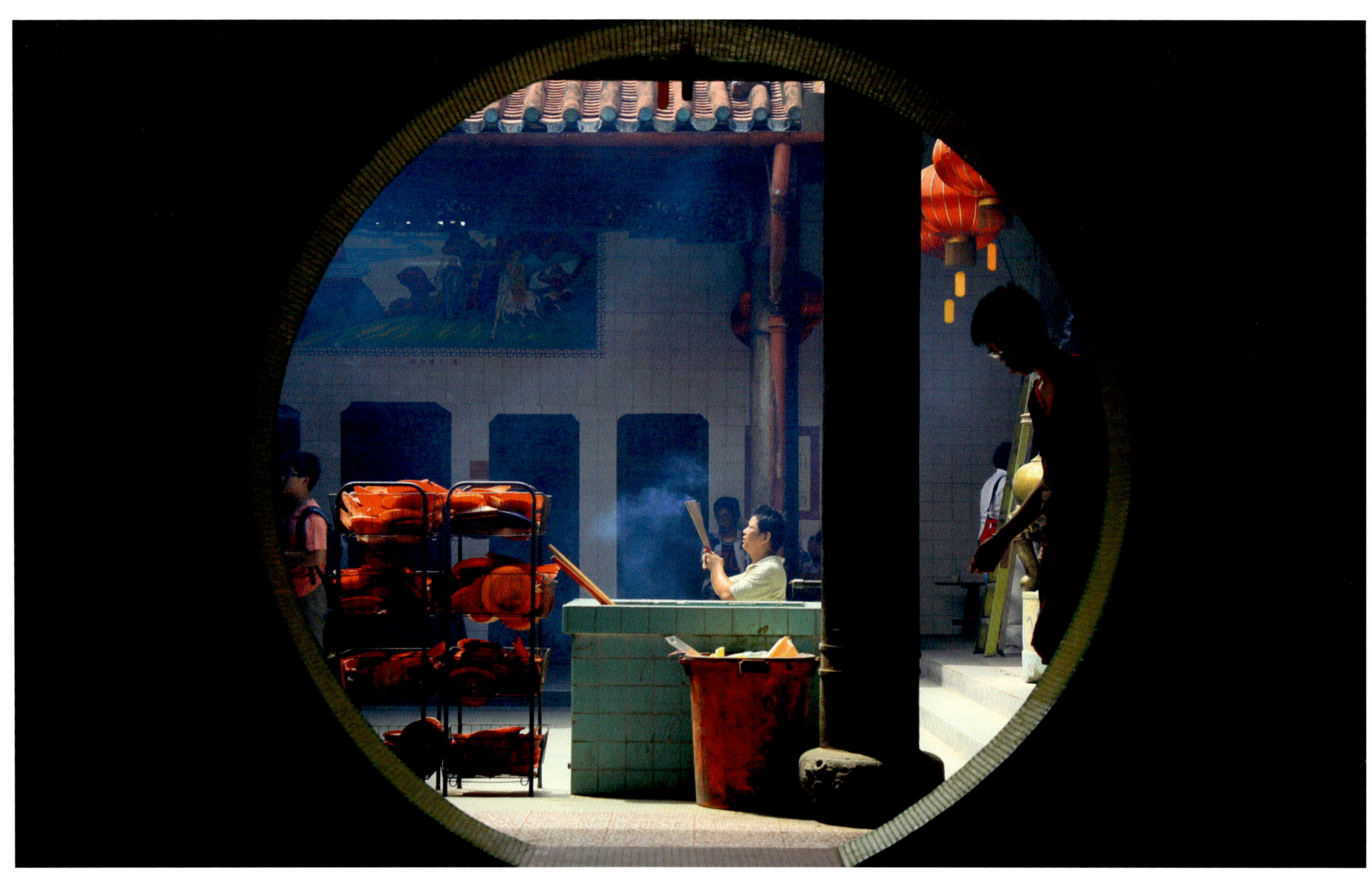

Malaysia / Daily life at Kuan Ying Teng temple

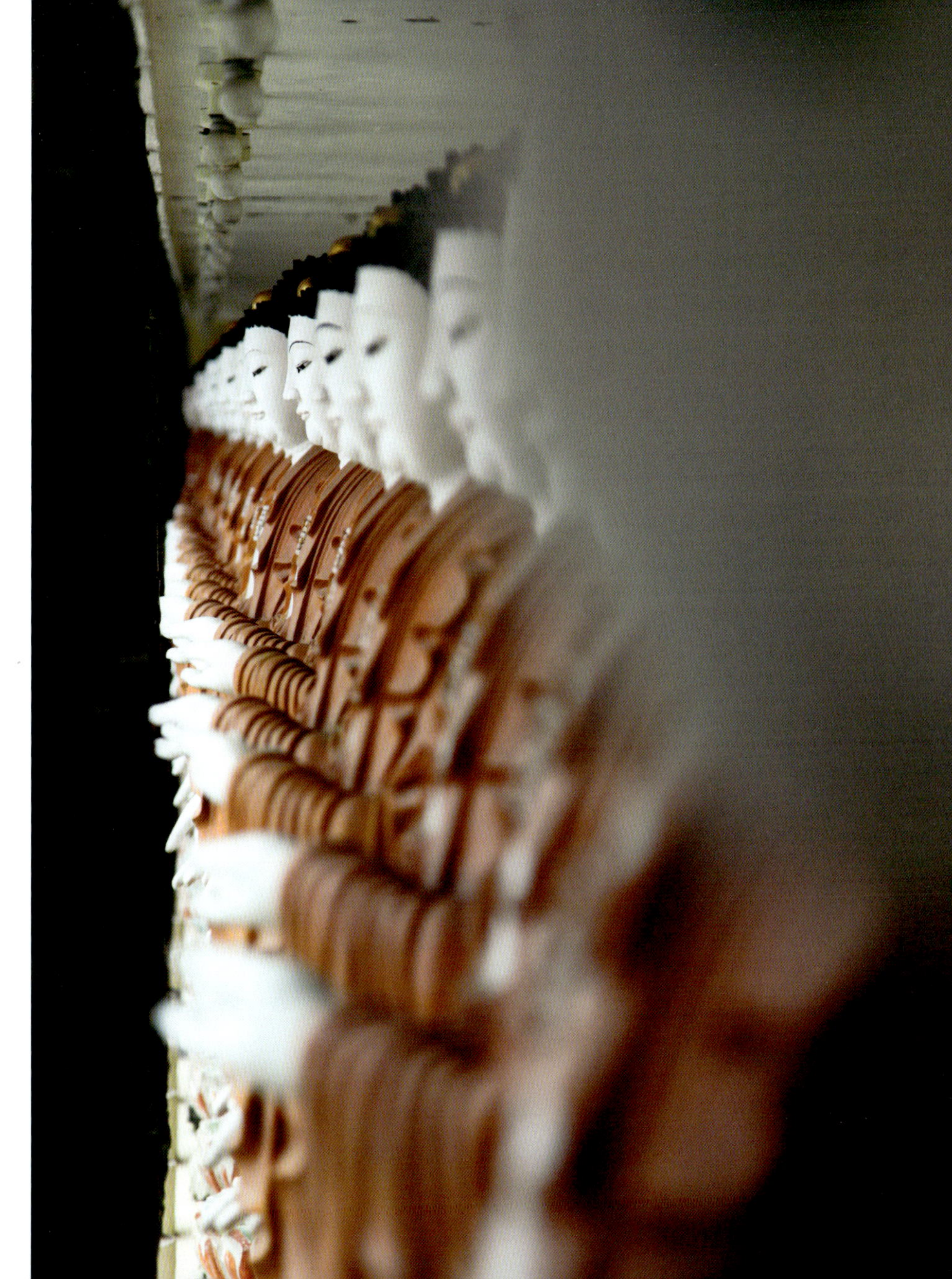

Malaysia / Bounty of Buddhas

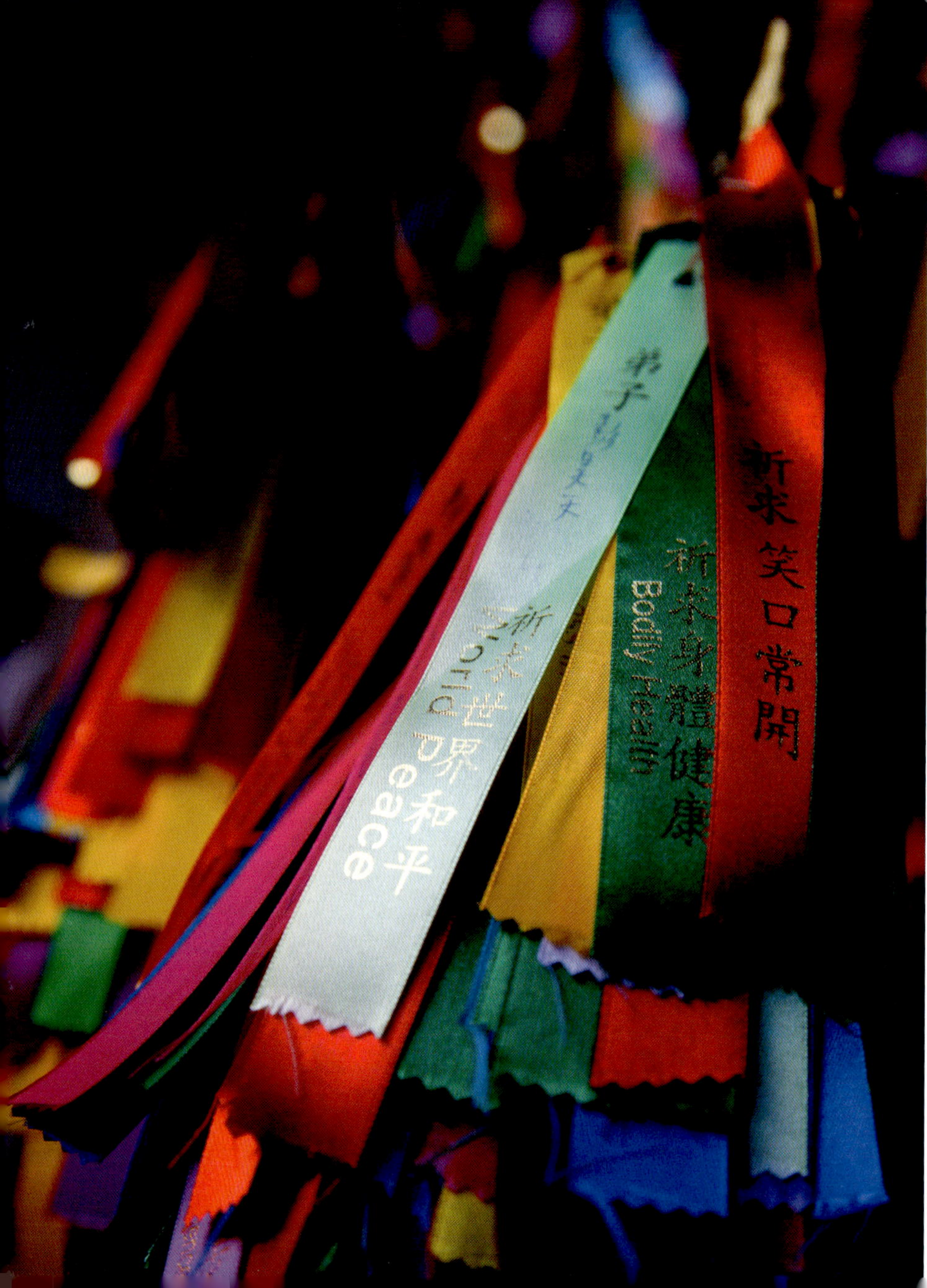

Malaysia / World peace

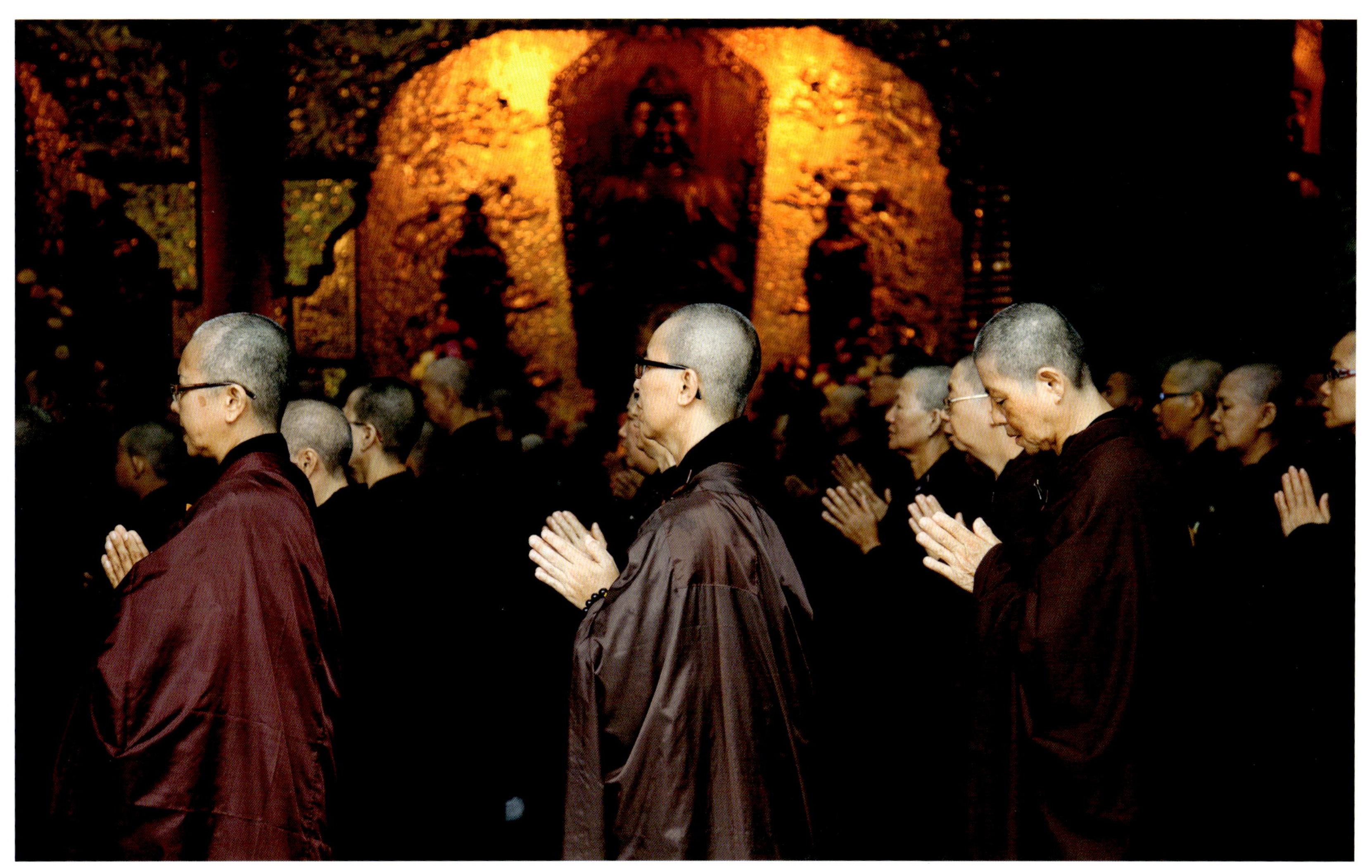

Malaysia / Rituals and rites

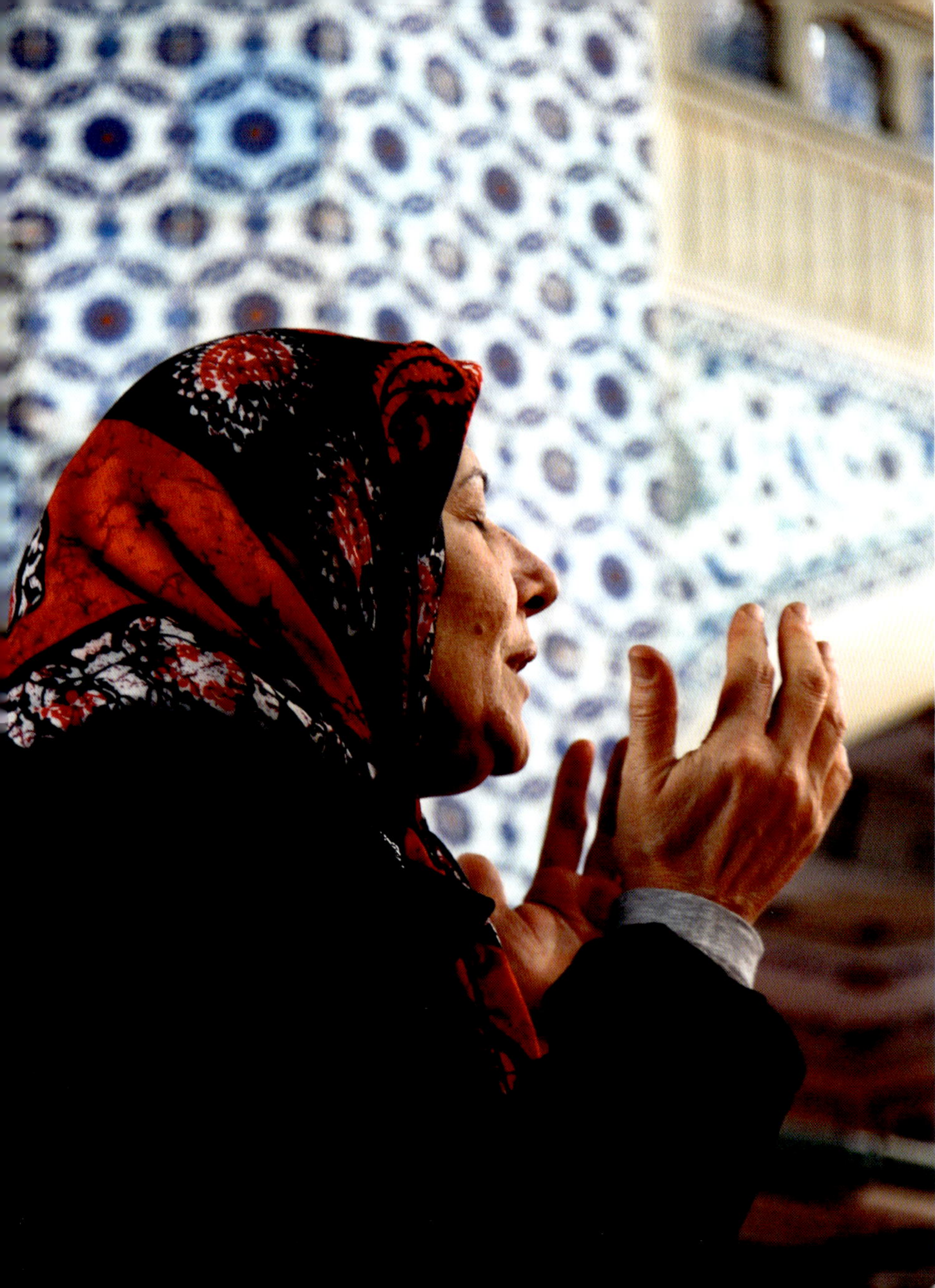

Turkey / Connect

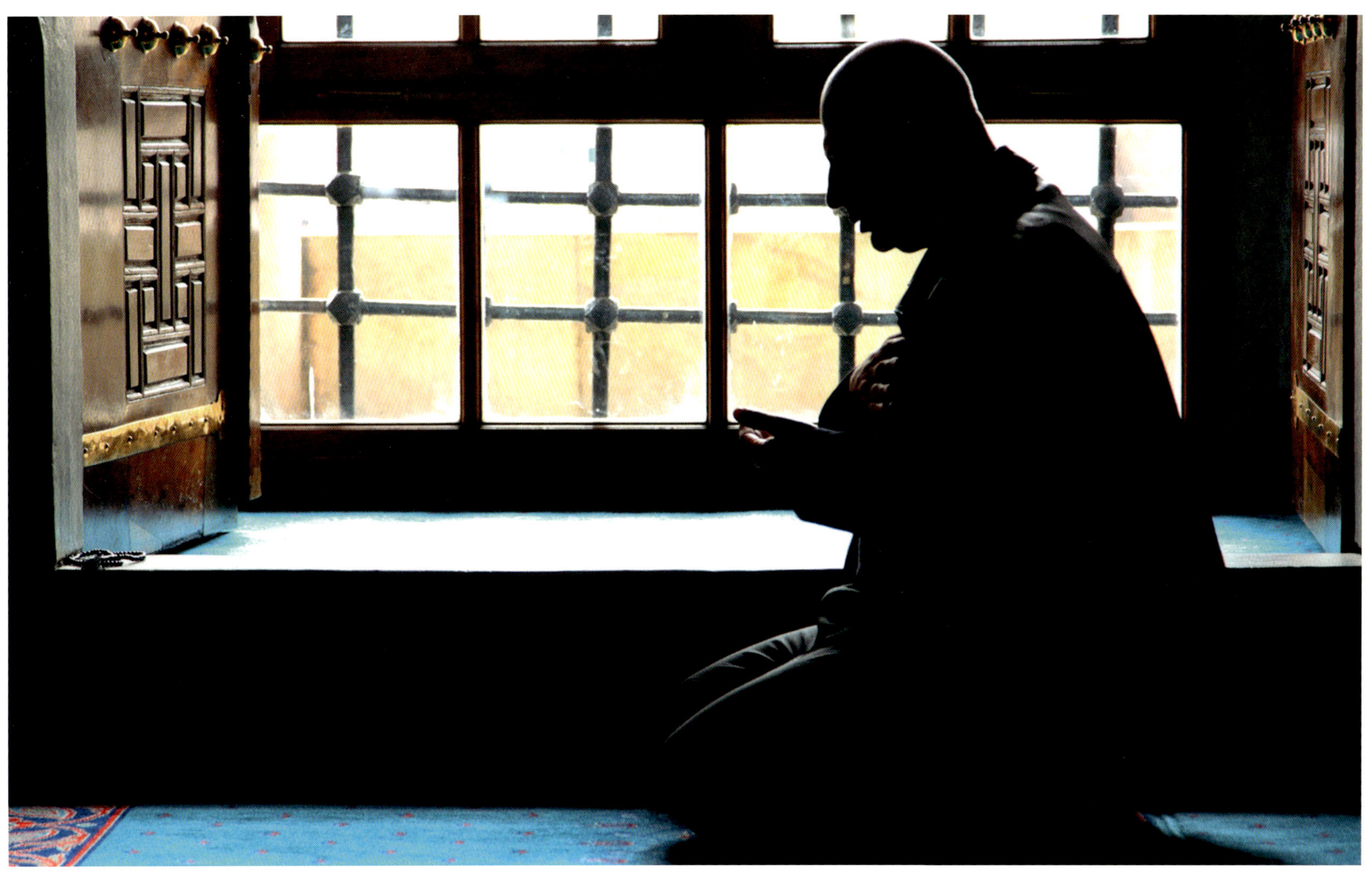

Turkey / Daily prayer

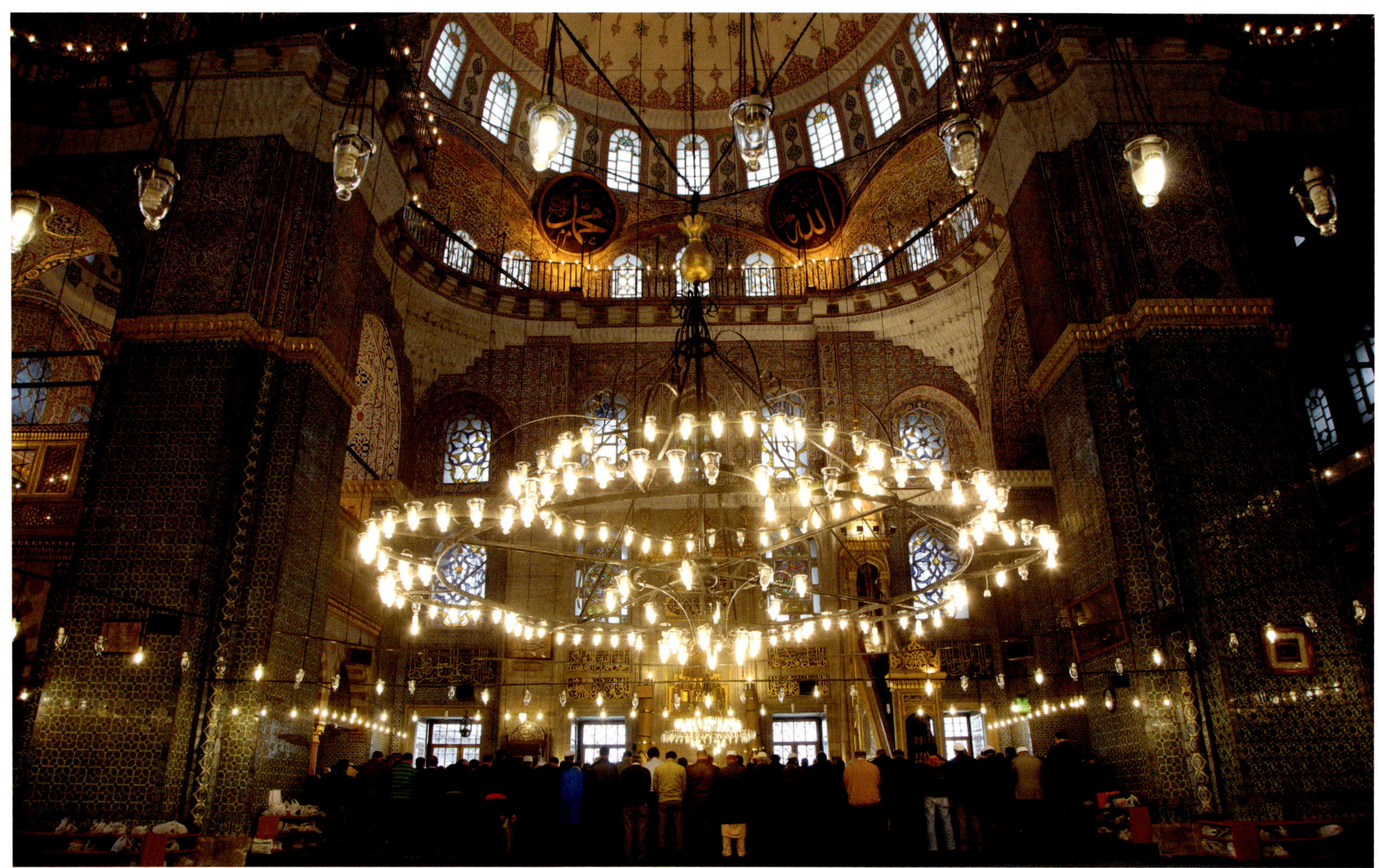

Turkey / Group worship

Georgia / Tsminda Sameba Church

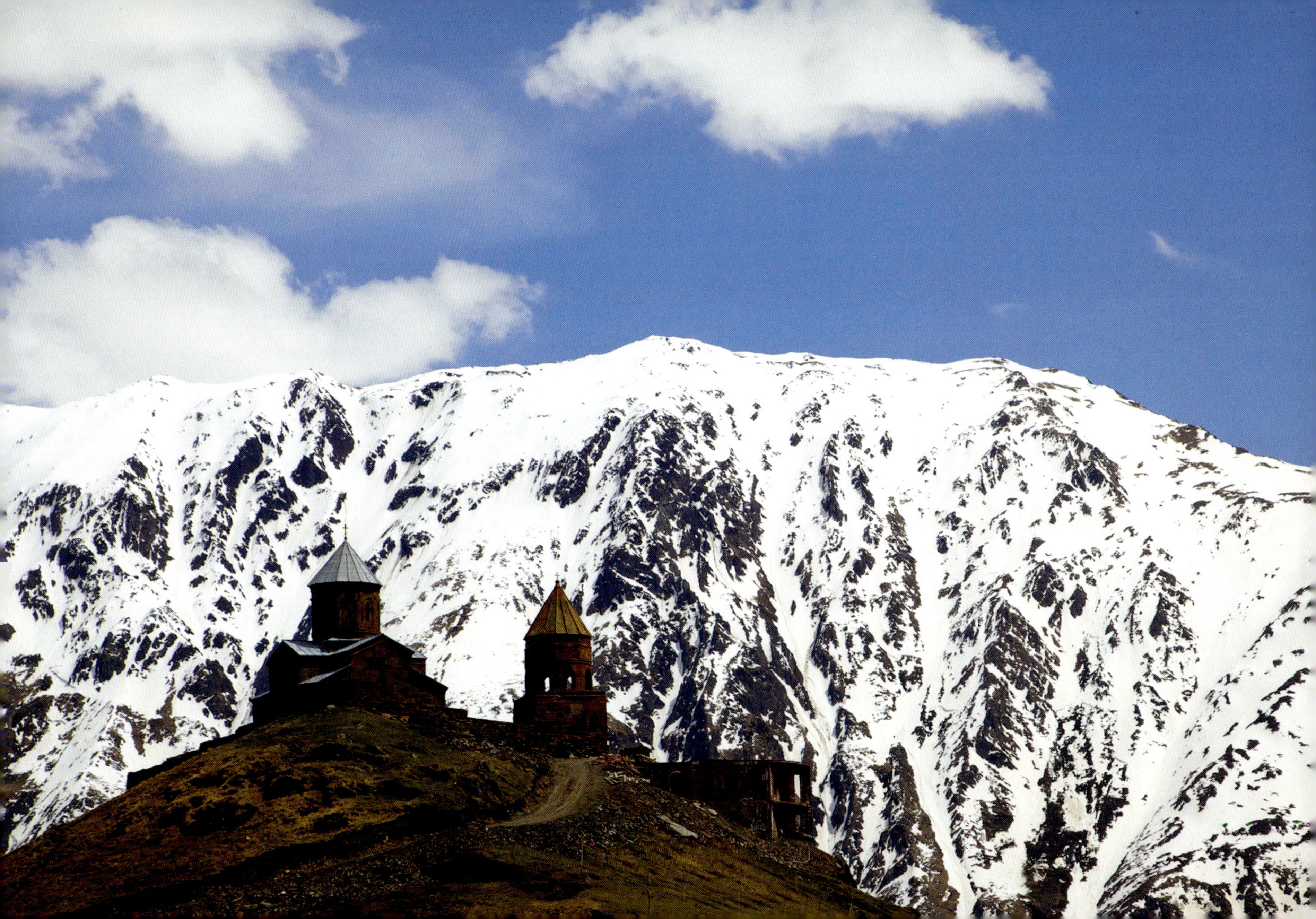

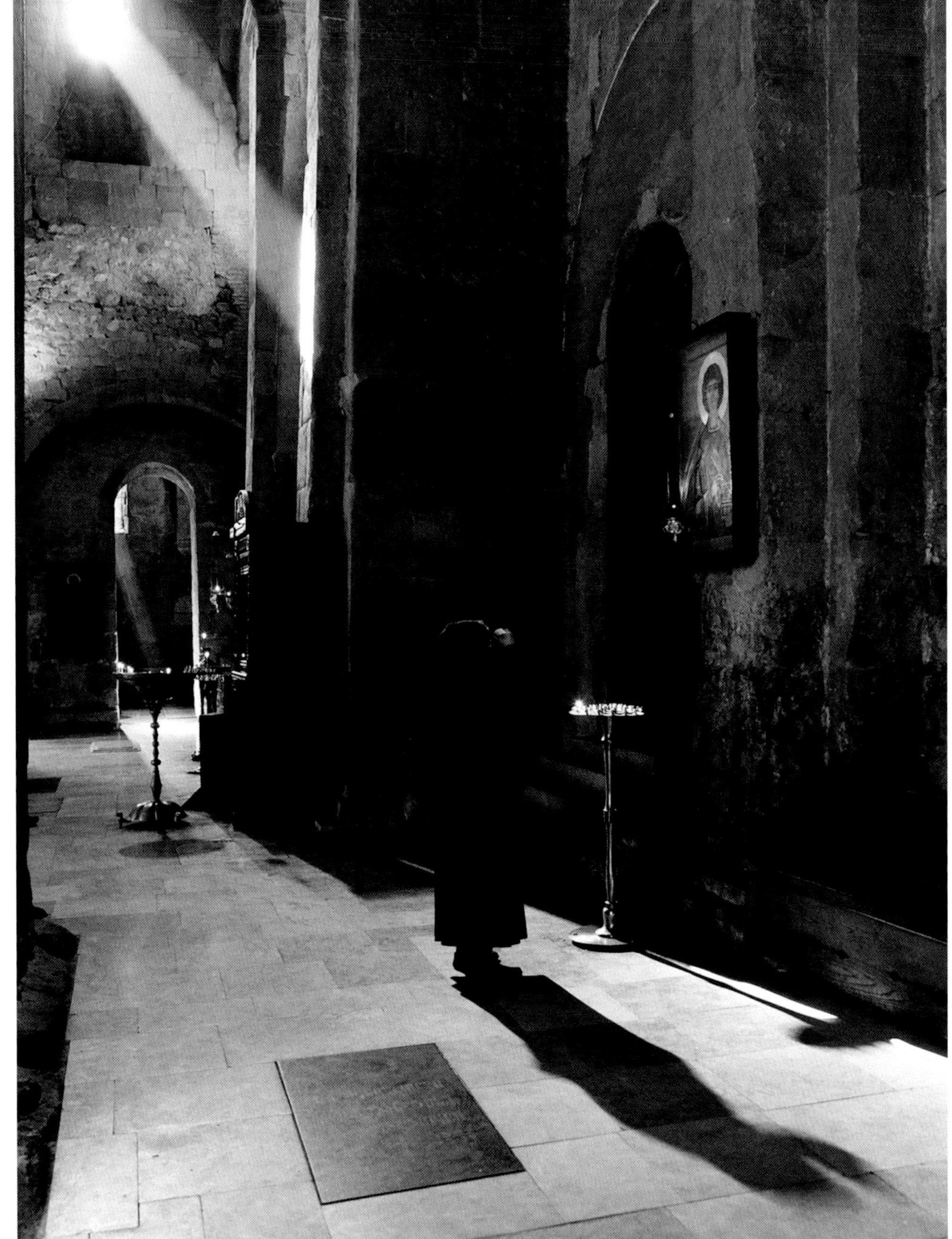

Georgia / Ray of hope

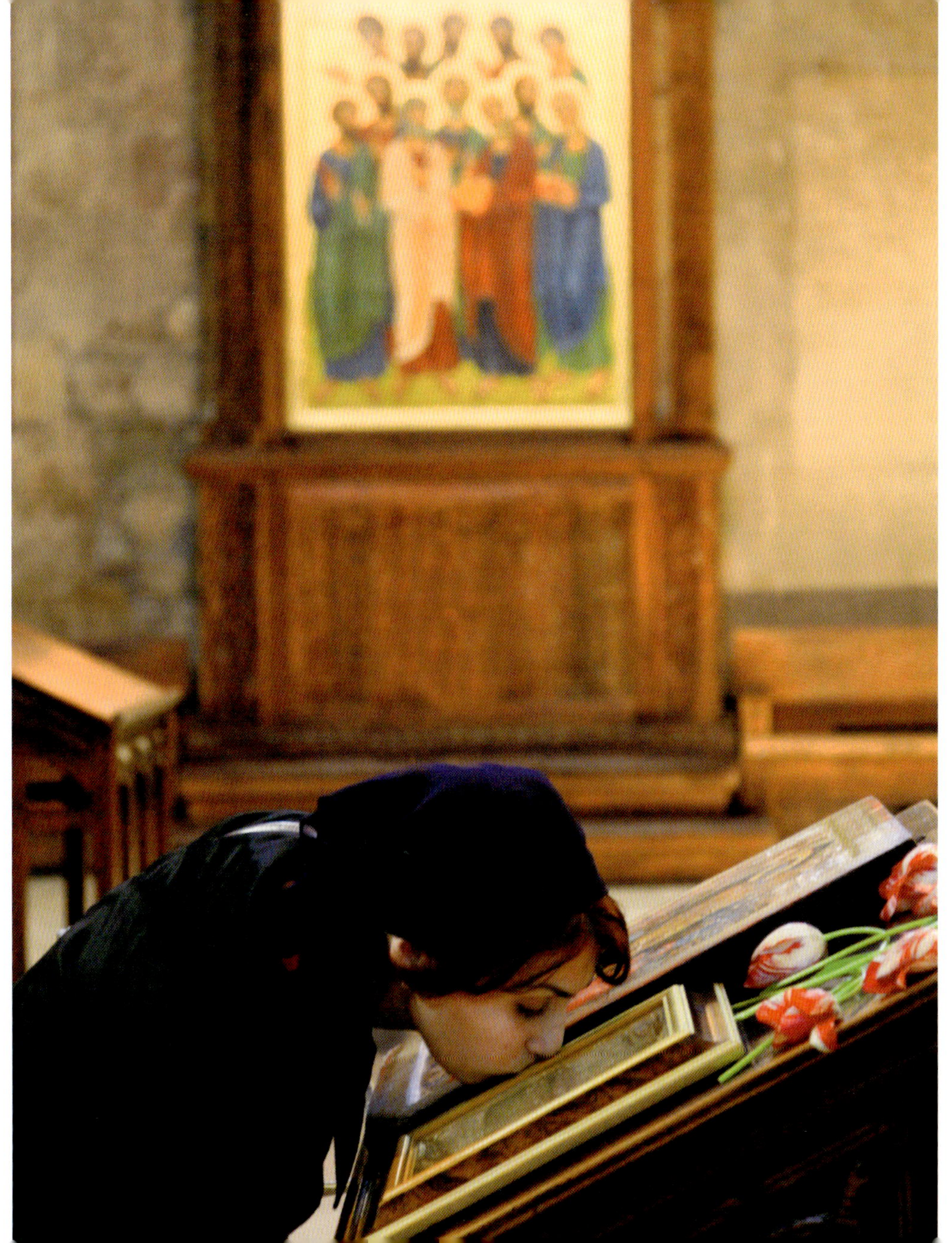

Georgia / Kissing God

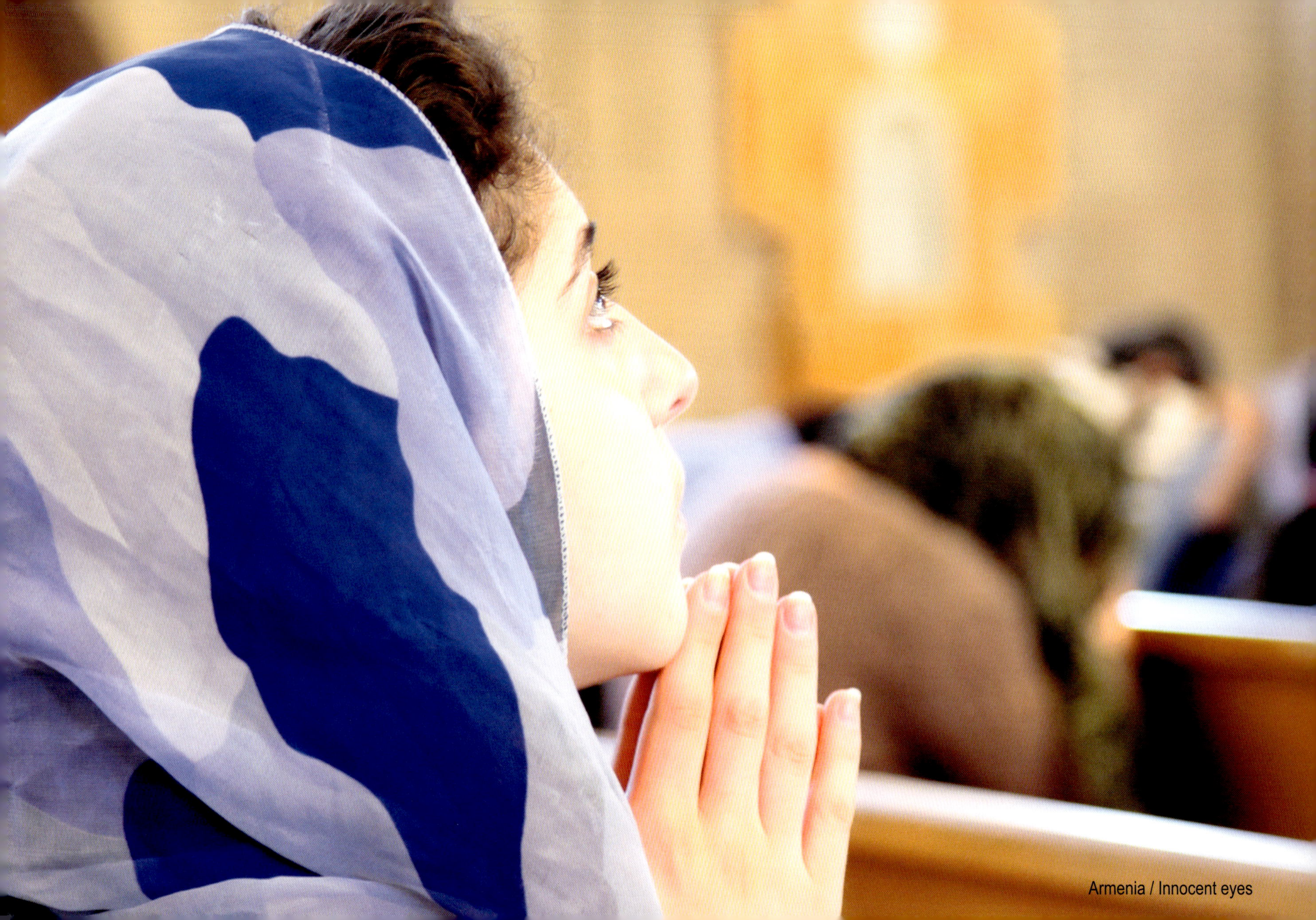

Armenia / Innocent eyes

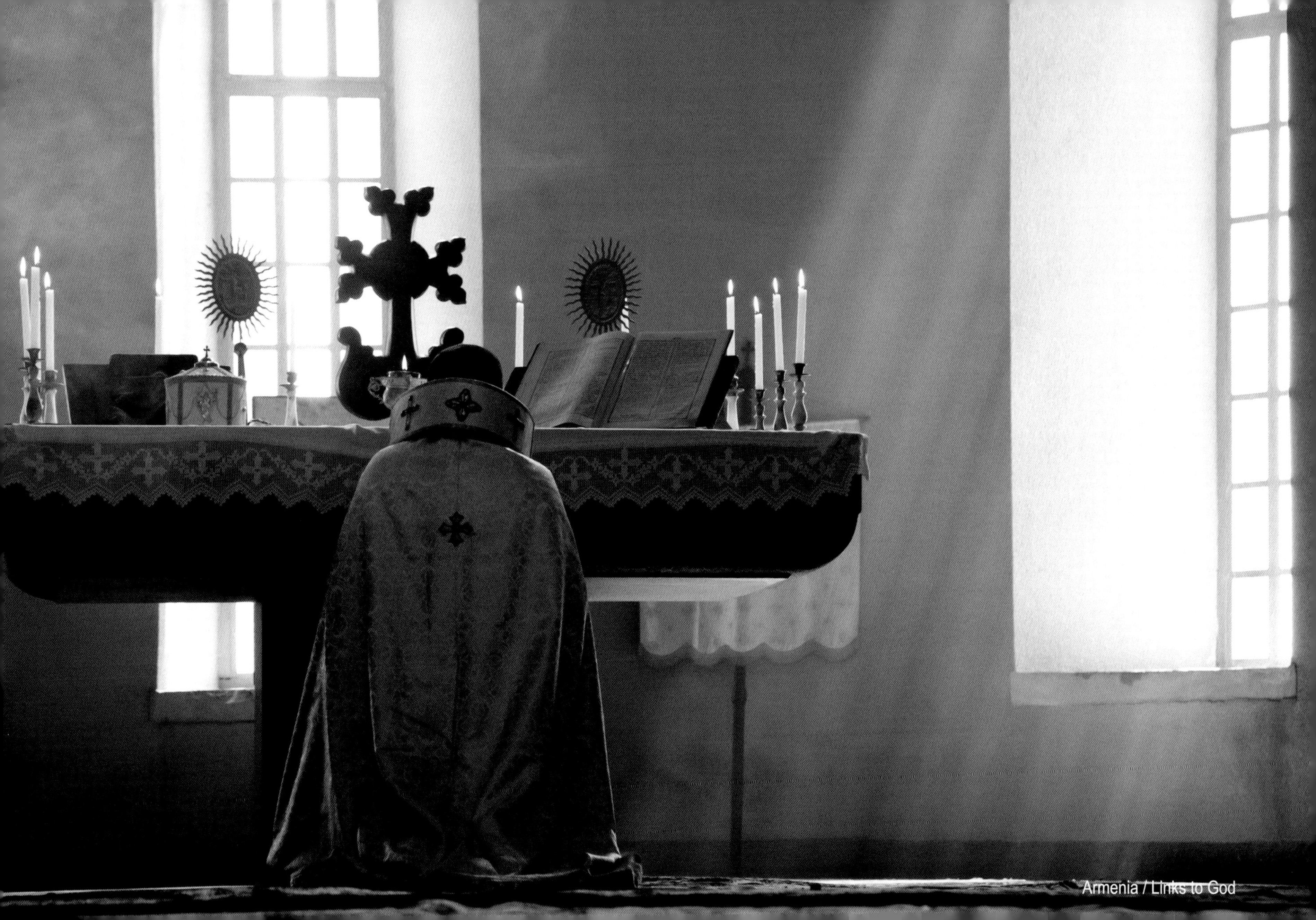
Armenia / Links to God

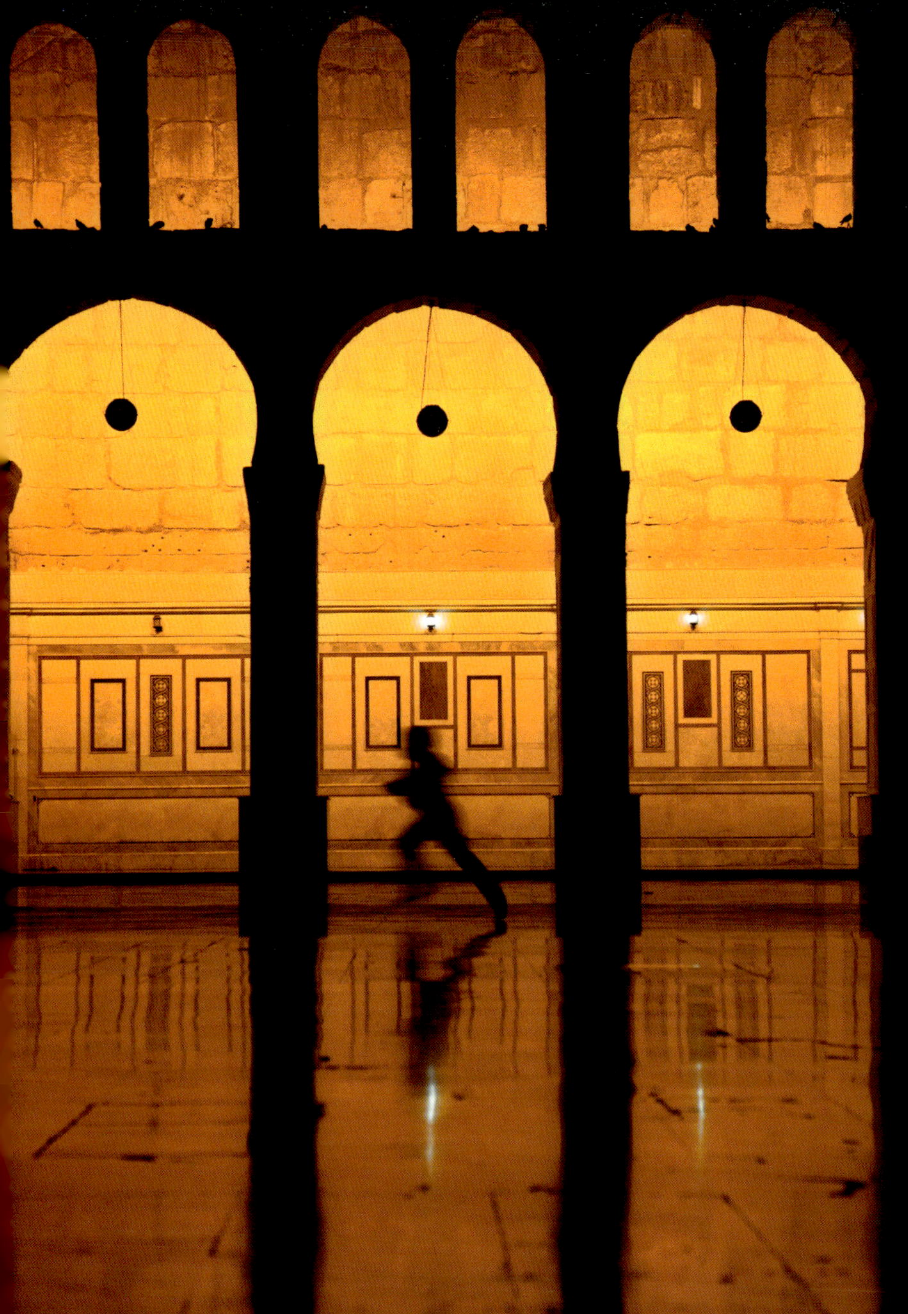

Syria / Run into the moment

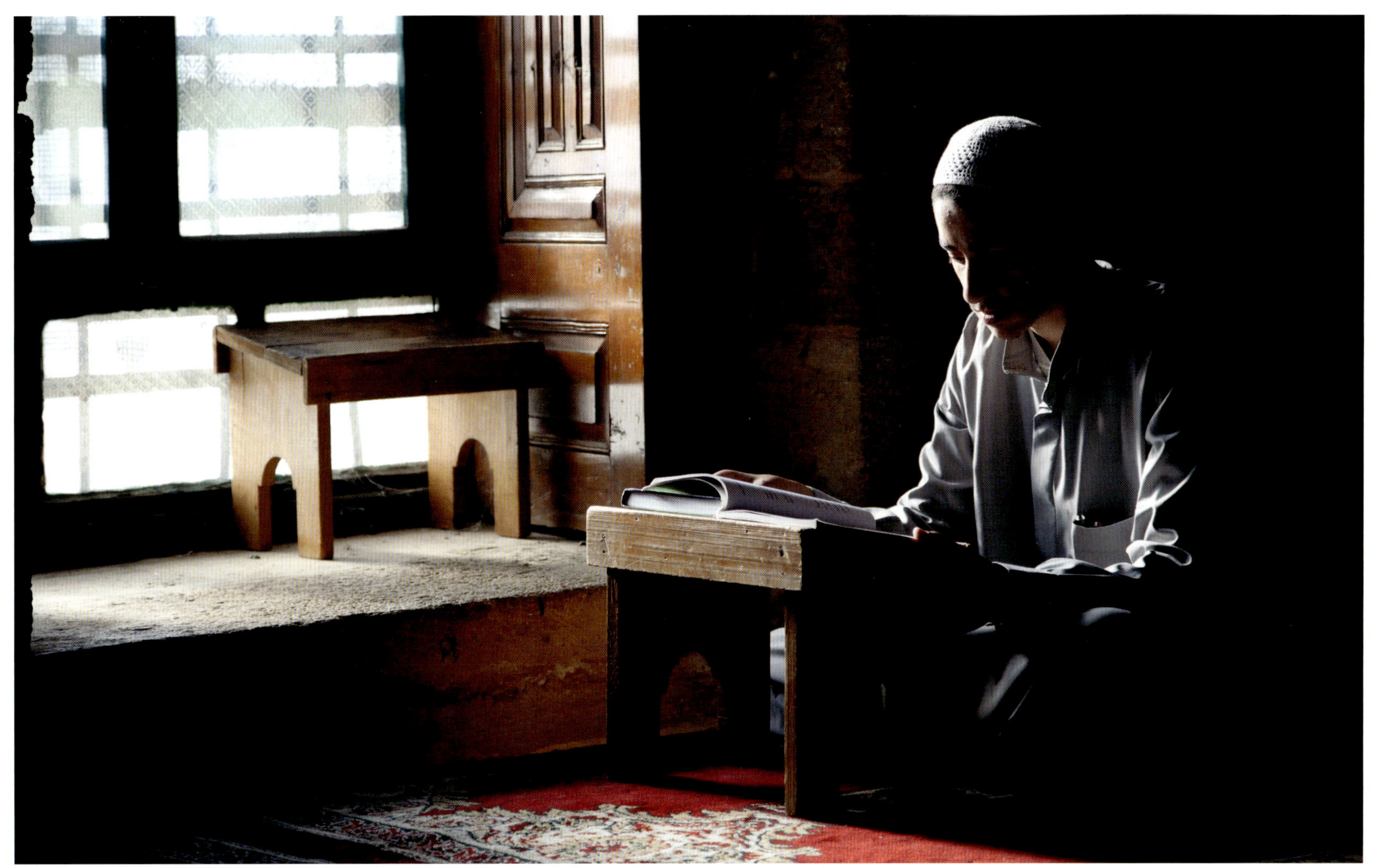

Lebanon / Holy time

no need to be confused…
no need to be complicated…

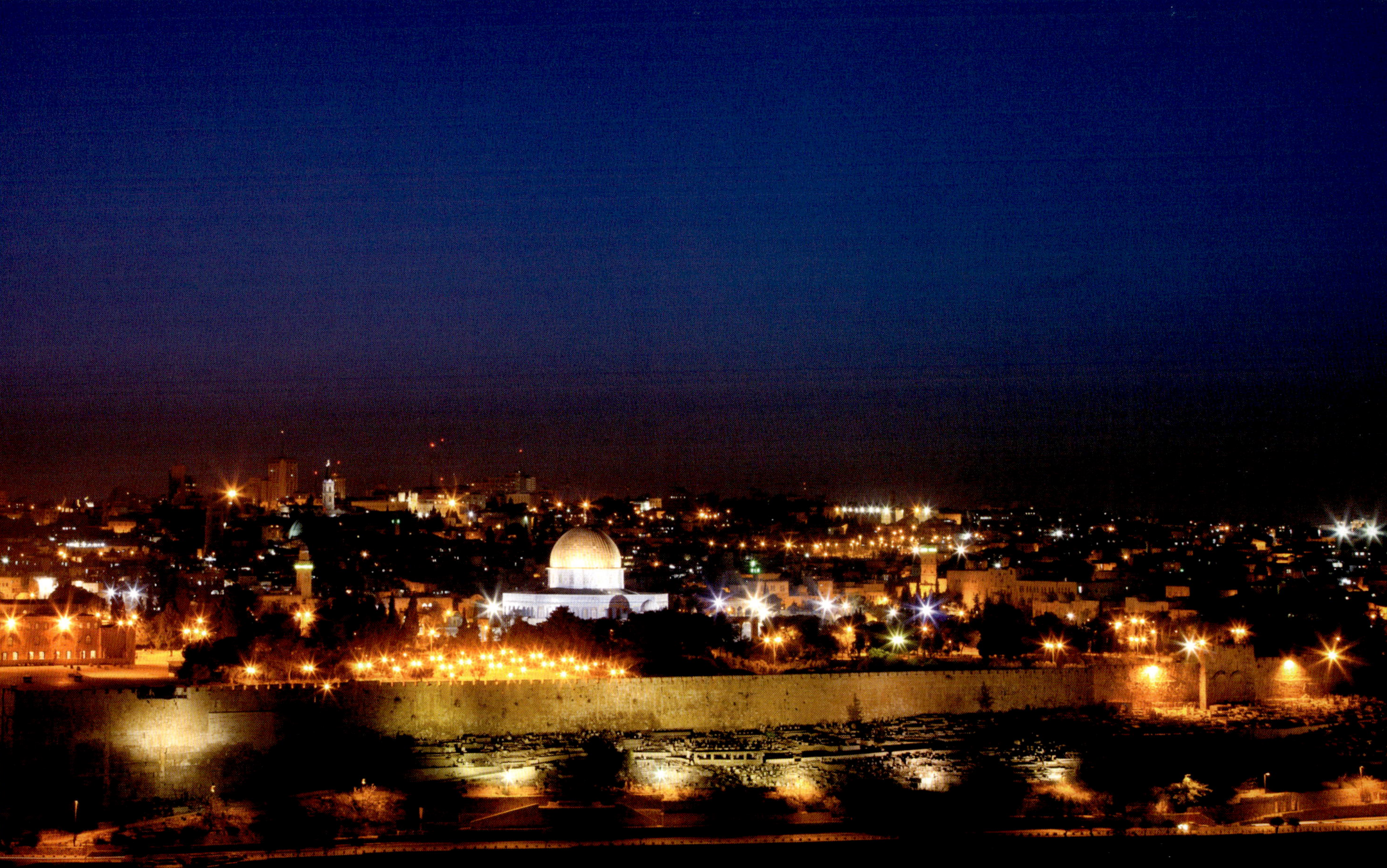

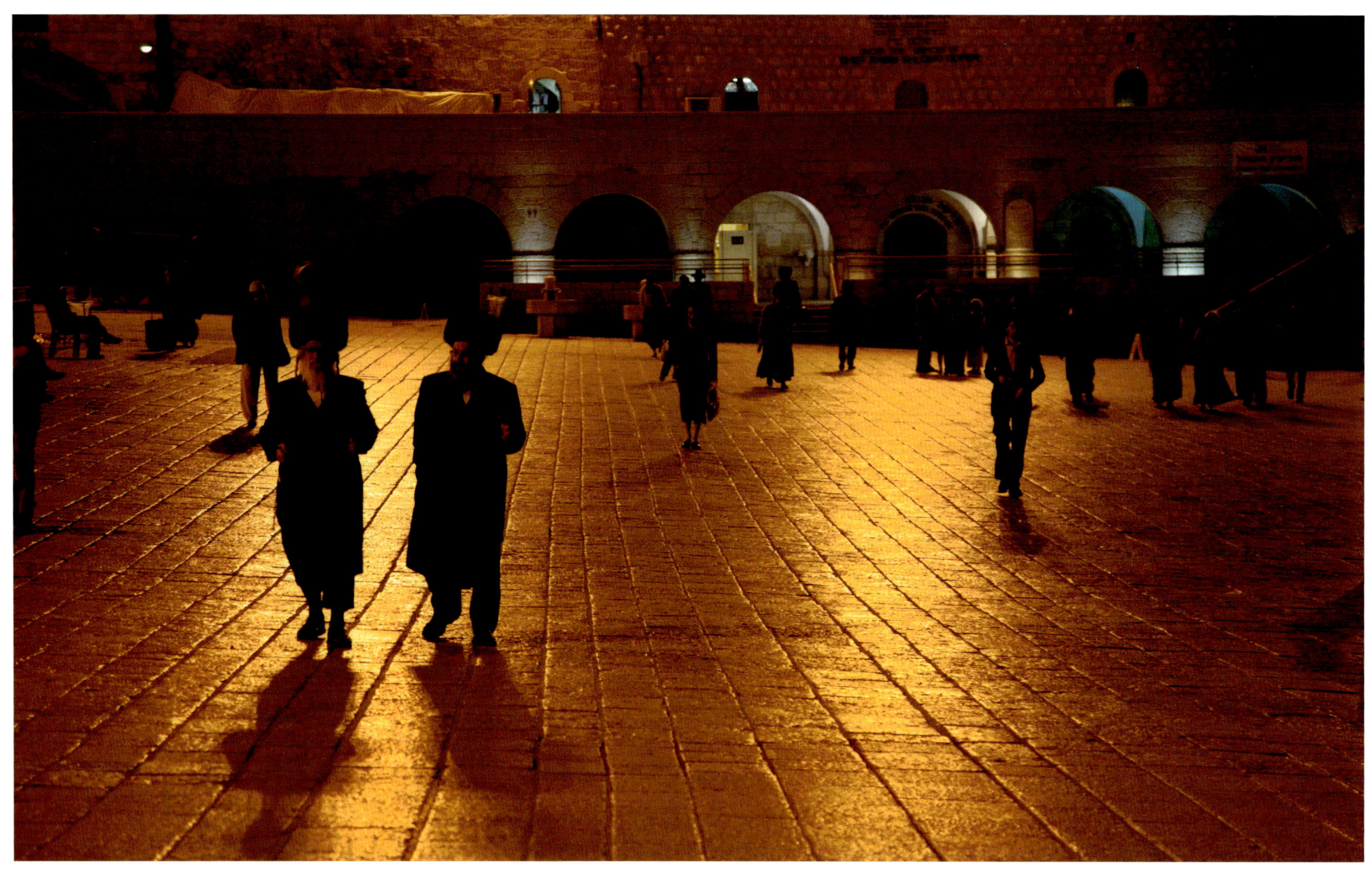

Israel / Daily life in Jerusalem

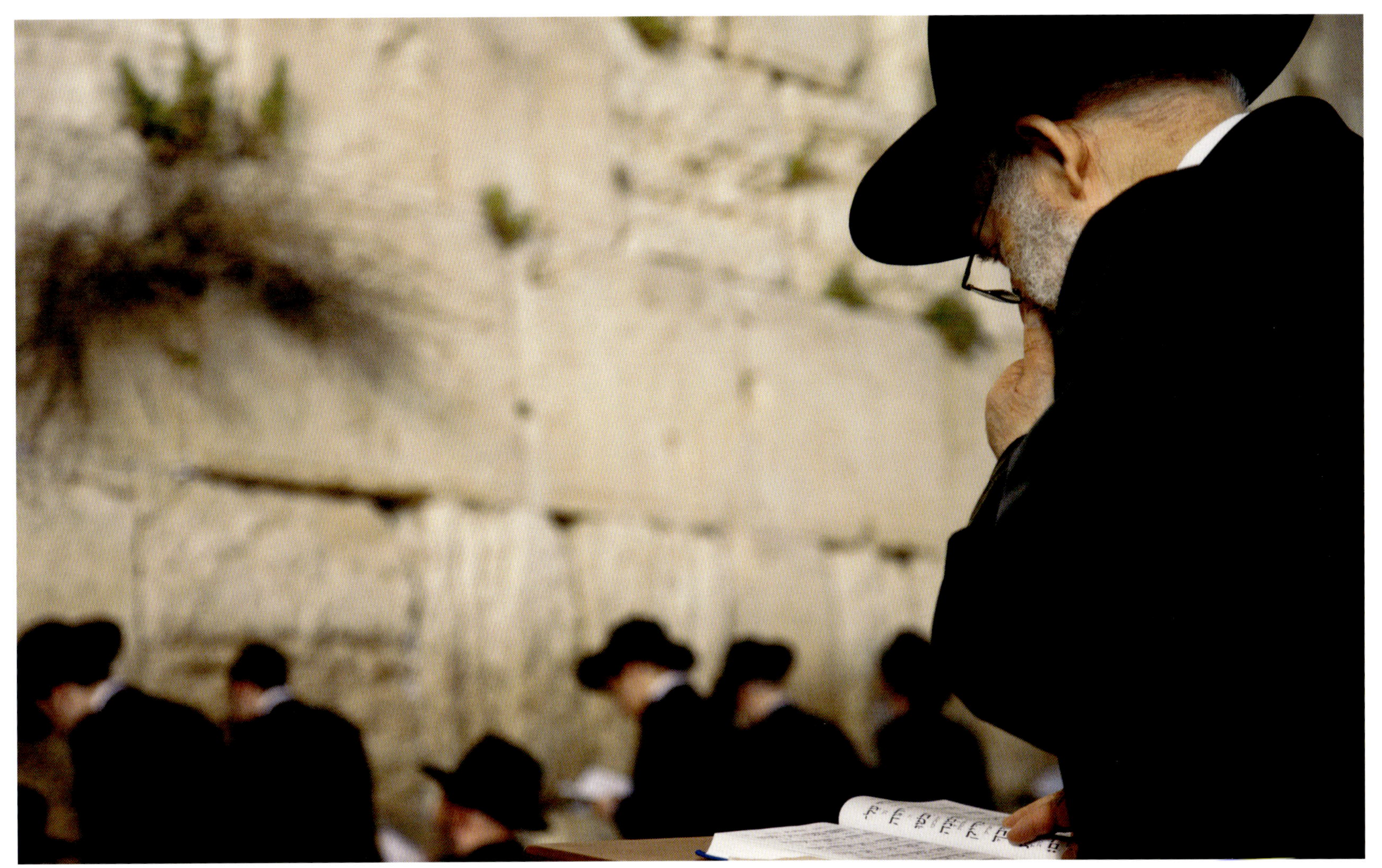

Israel / The wailing wall

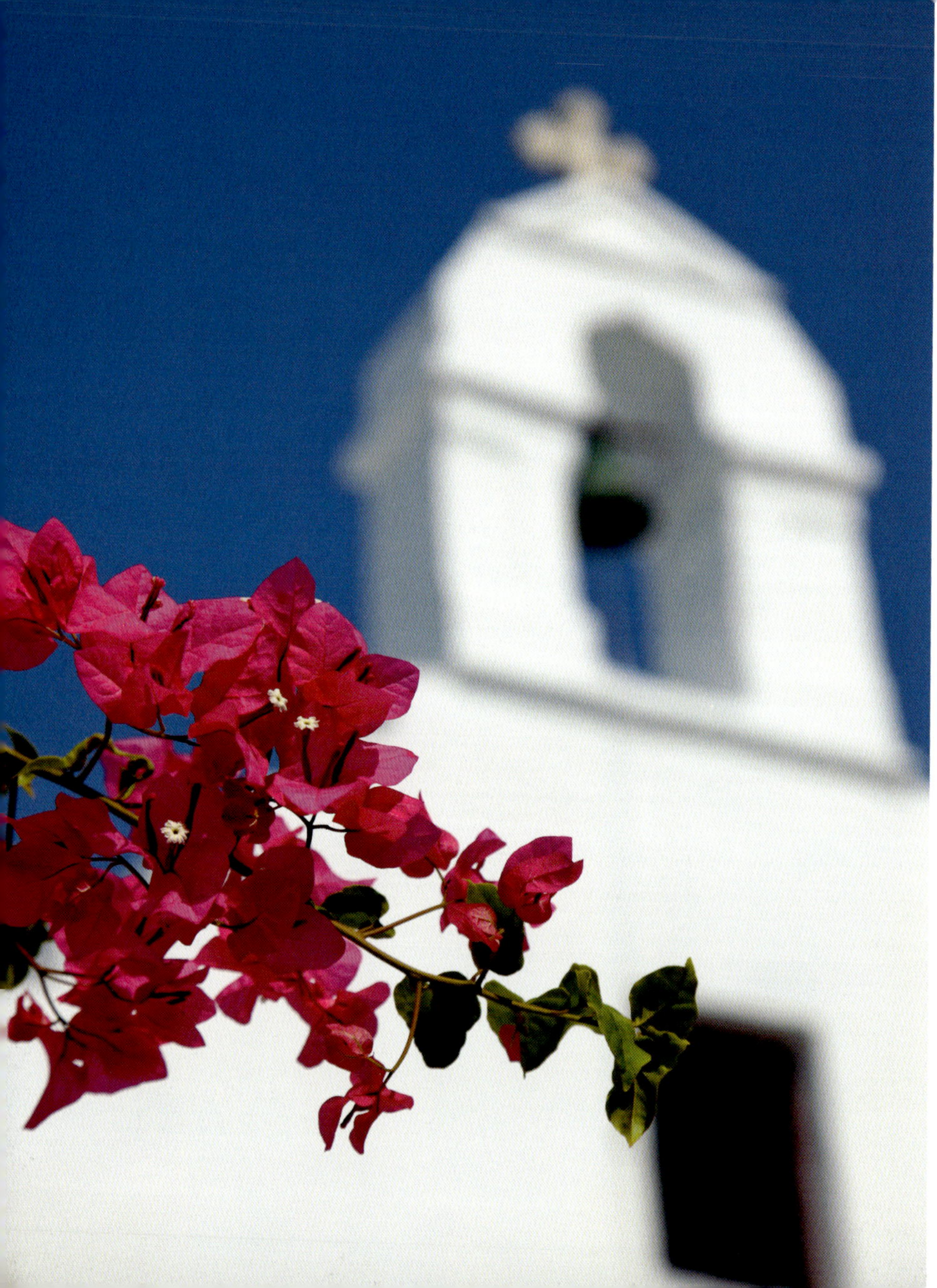

Greece / Bougainvillea and a white belfry

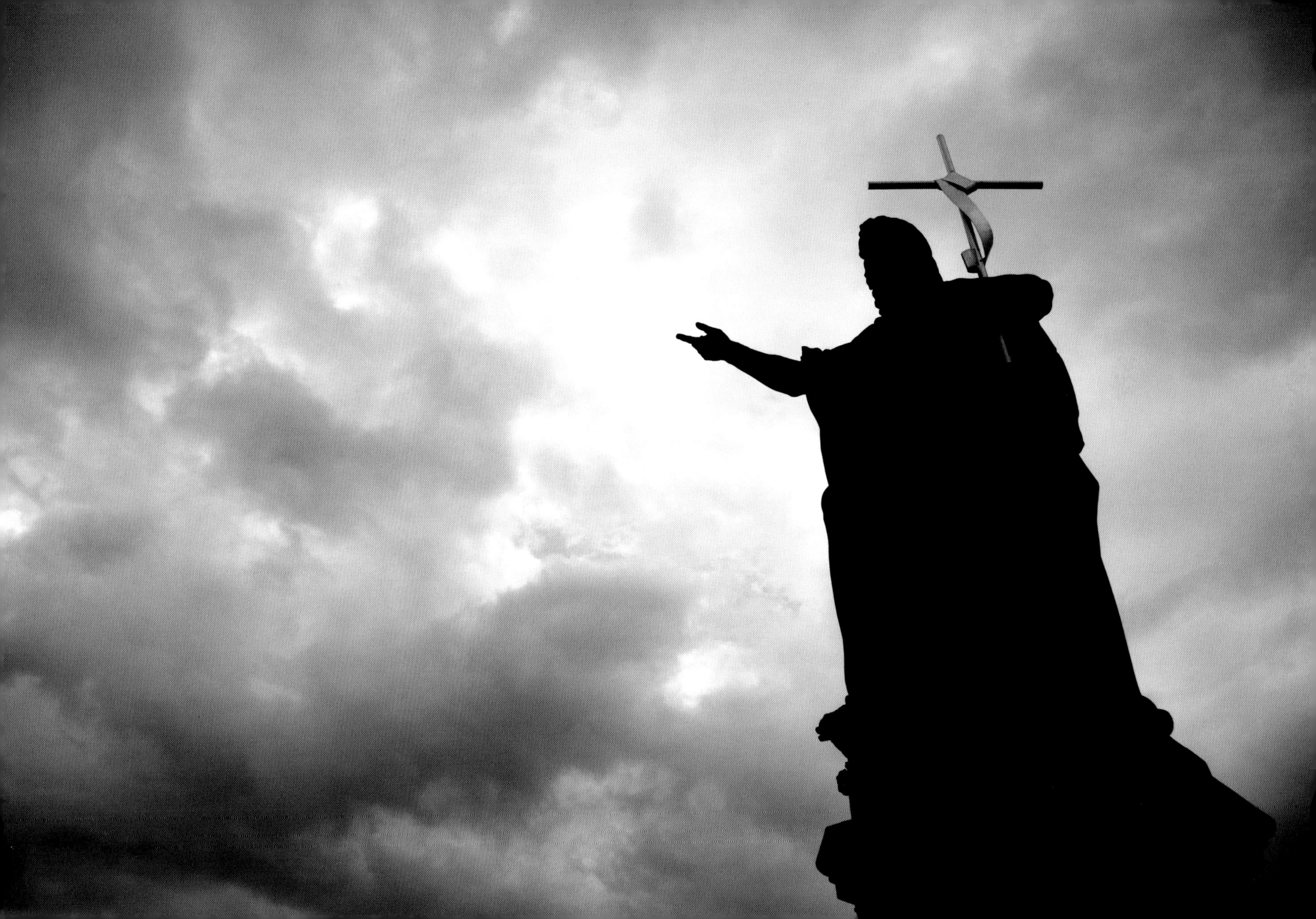

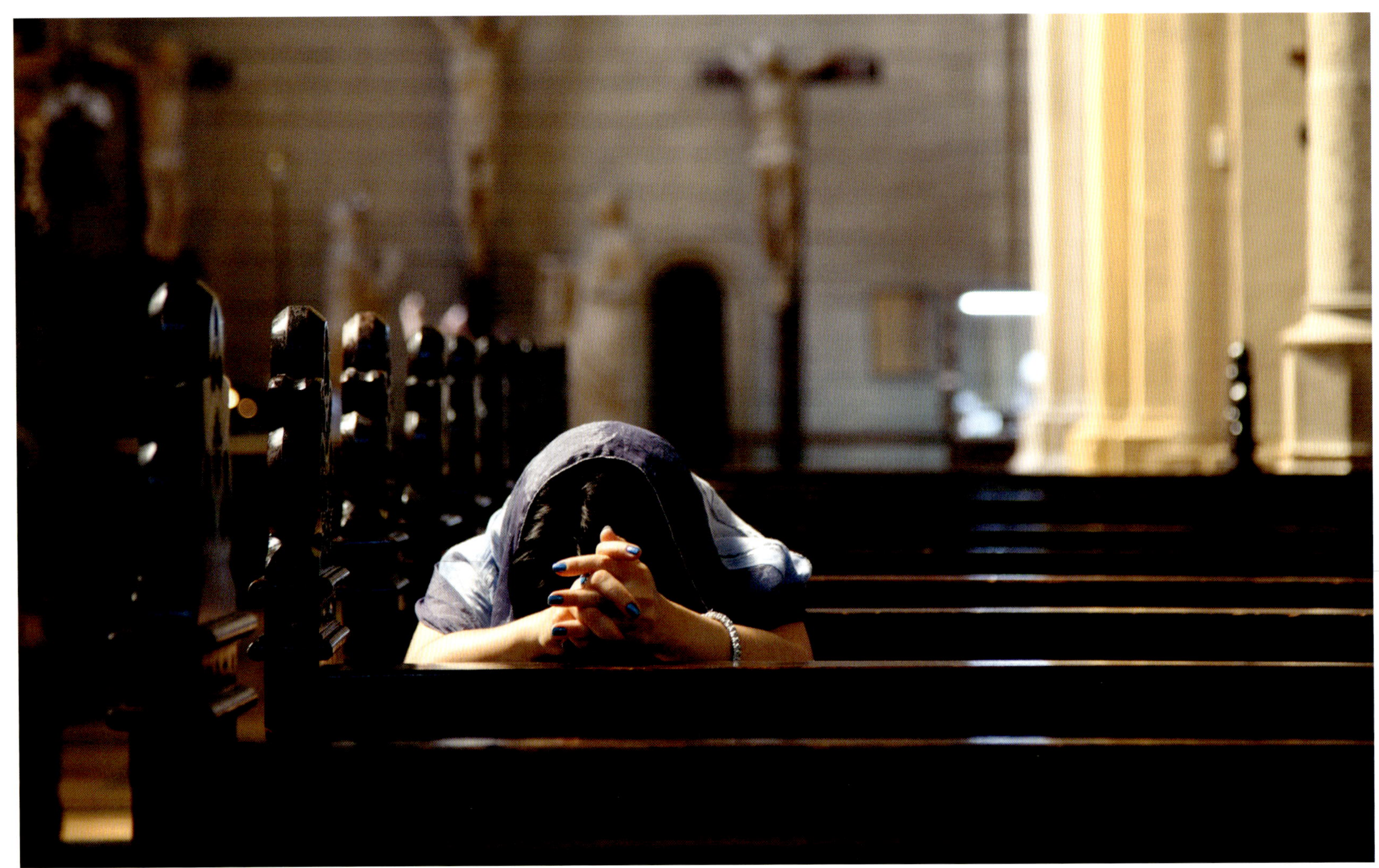

Croatia / Lord's prayer

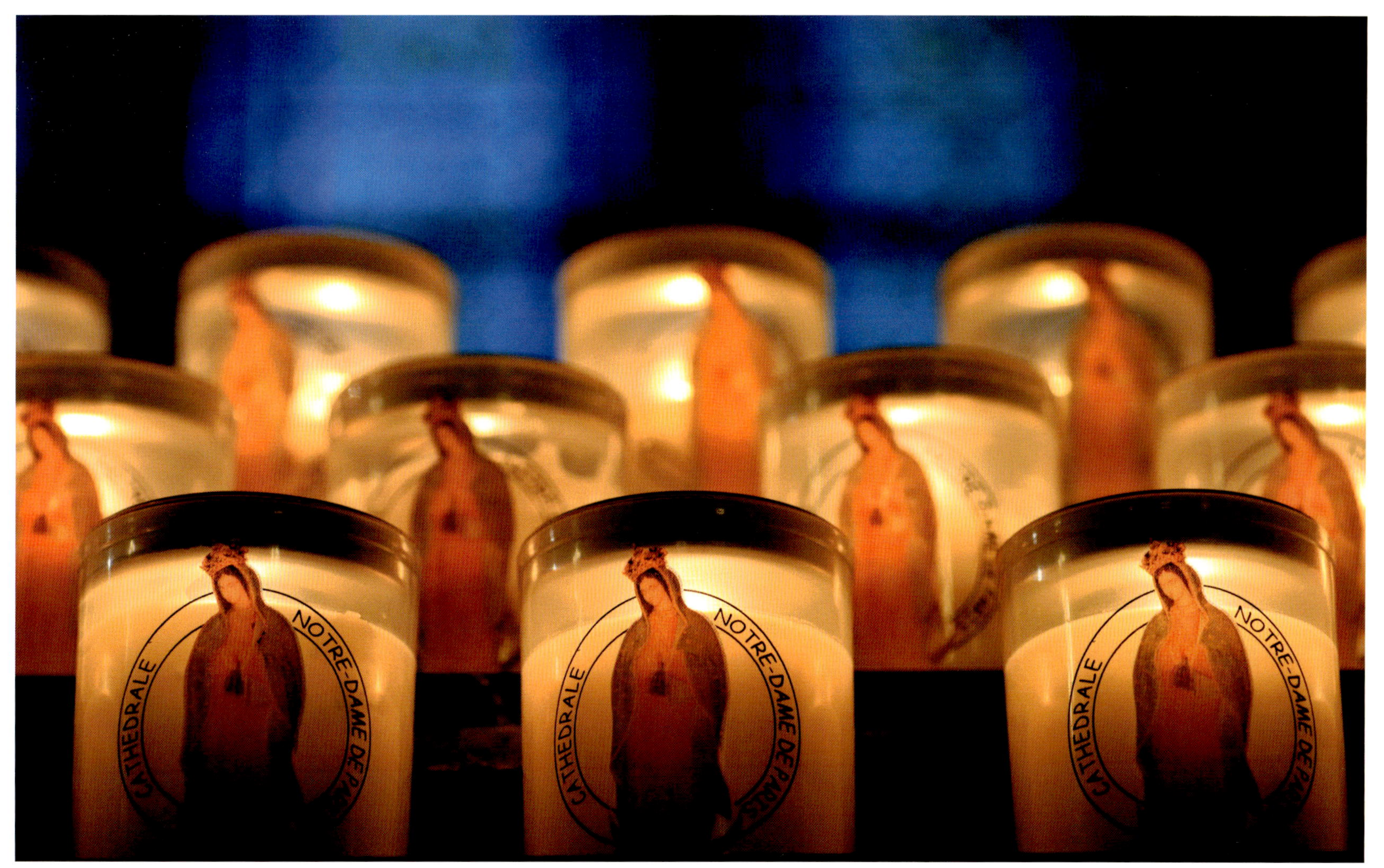

France / Sacred candlelight

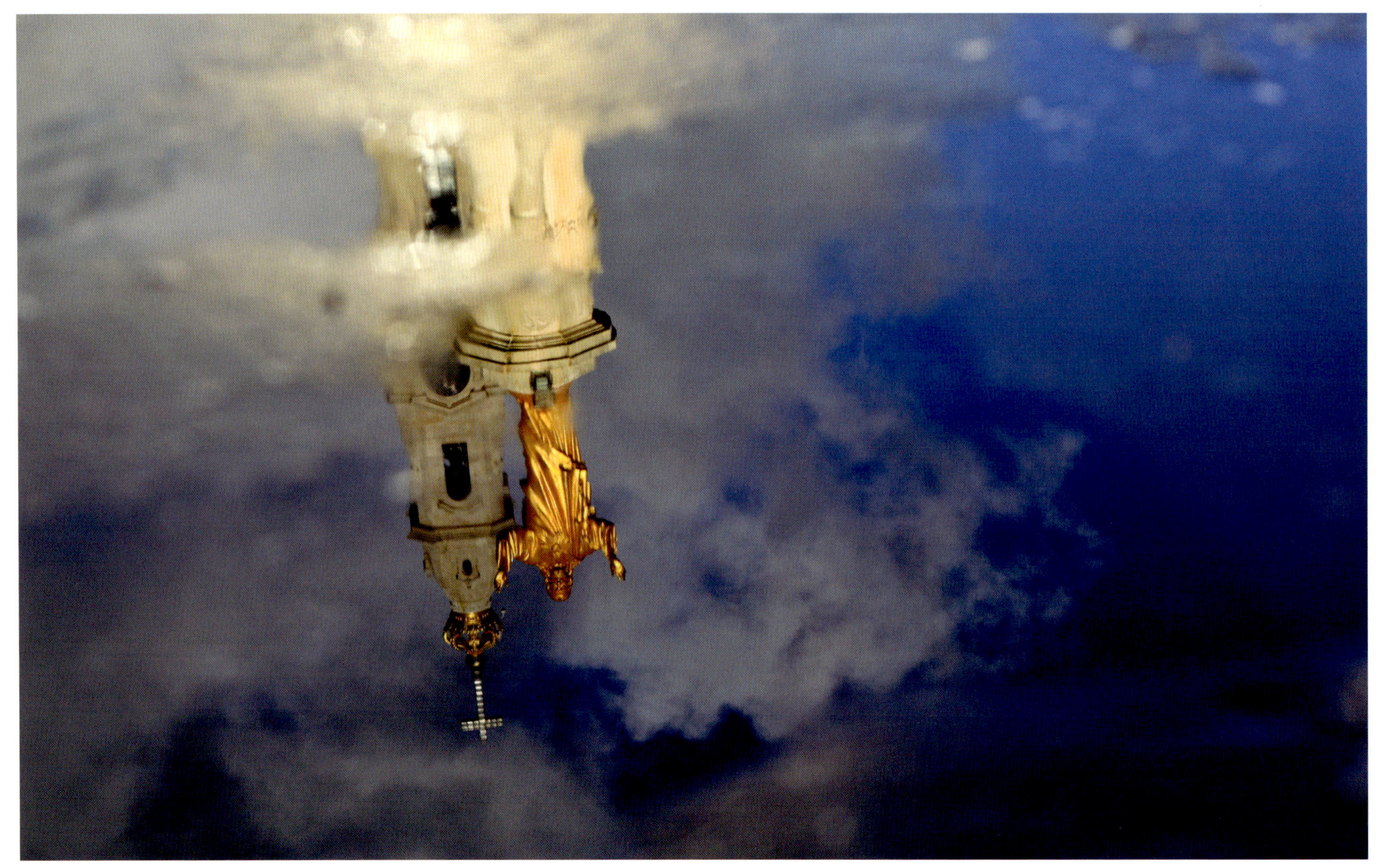

Portugal / Fatima after rain

Portugal / Cristo-Rei beyond the Tagus river

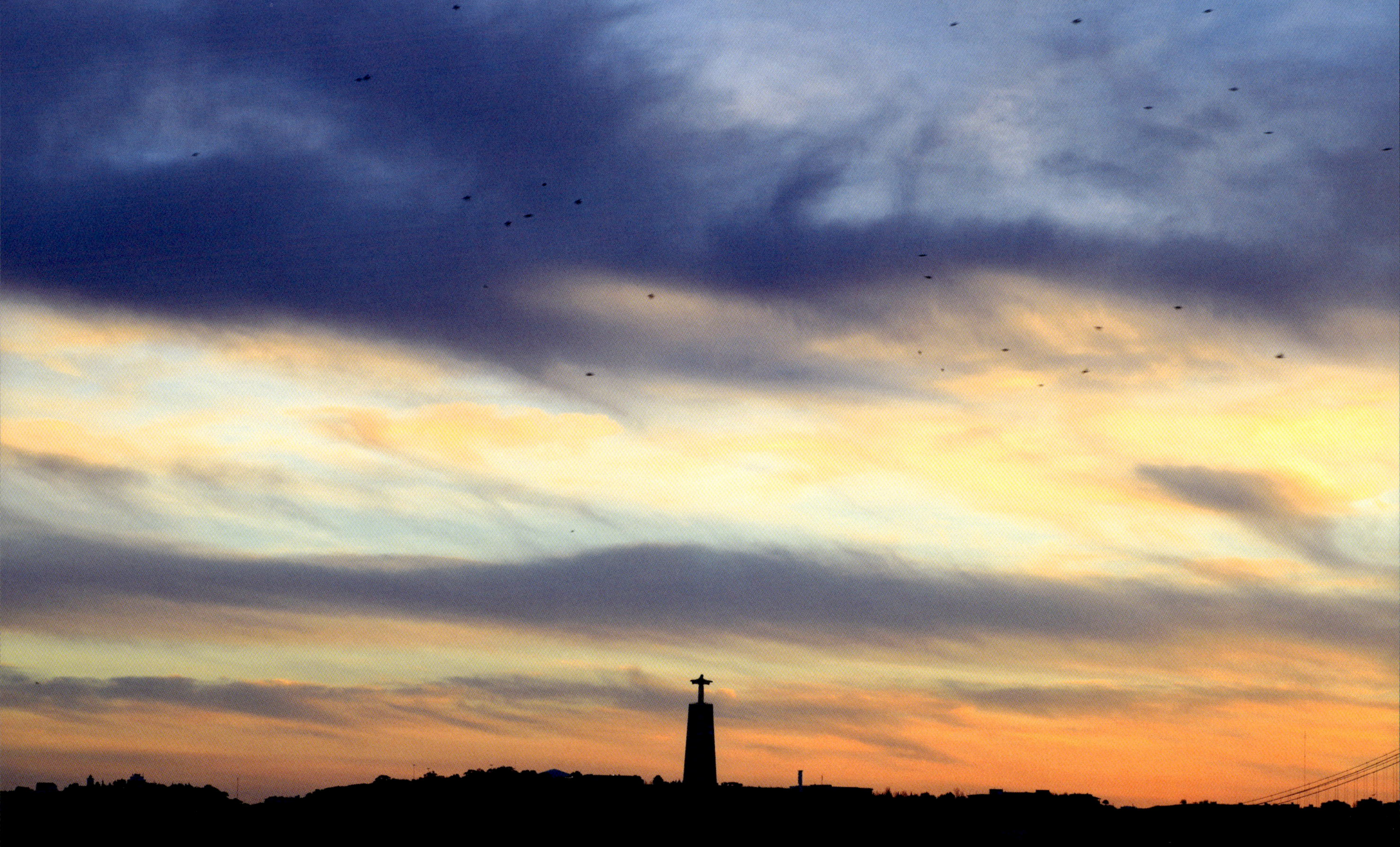

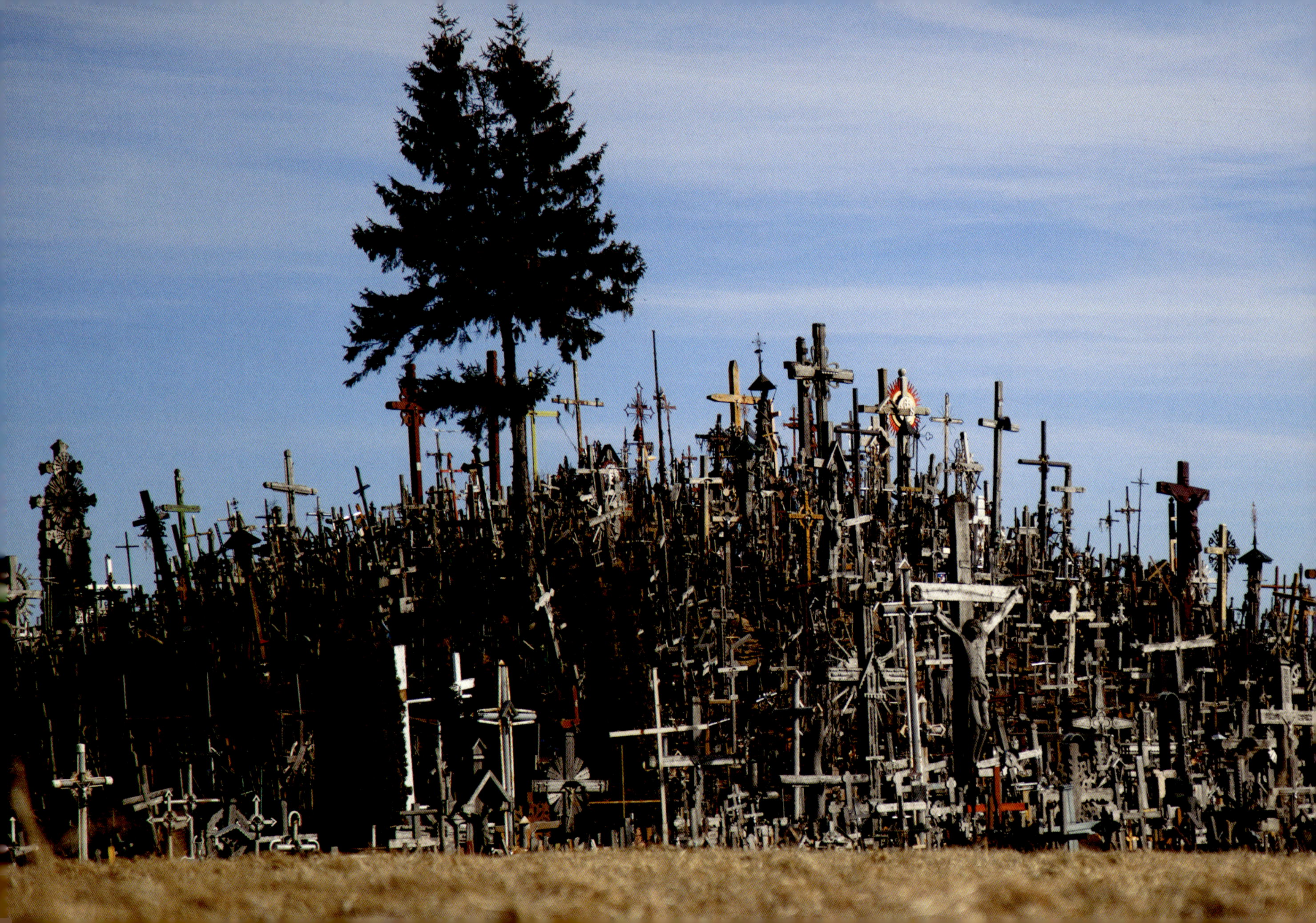

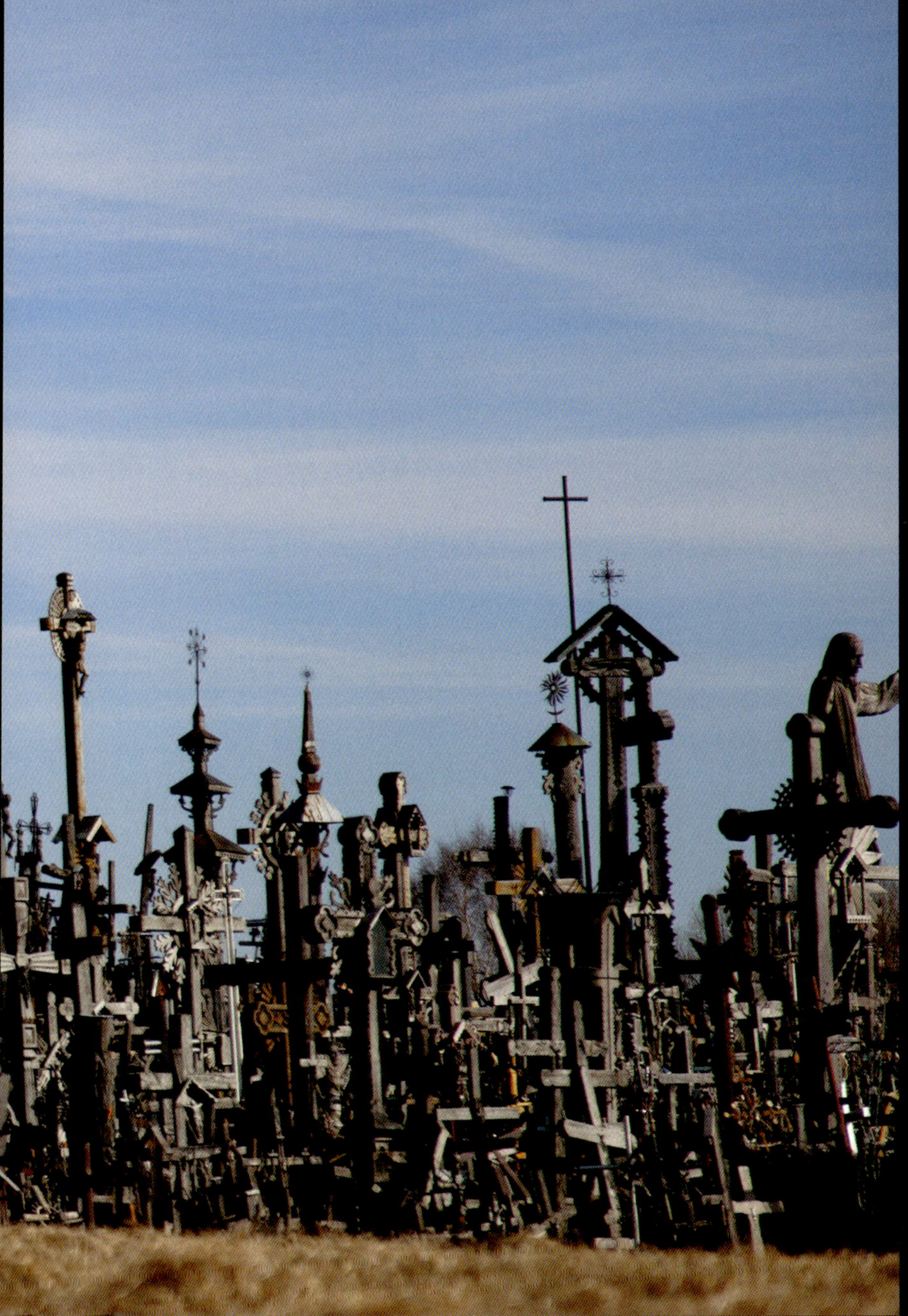

just be simple like a falling leaves,
river and flow of nature

Lithuania / Hill of the cross

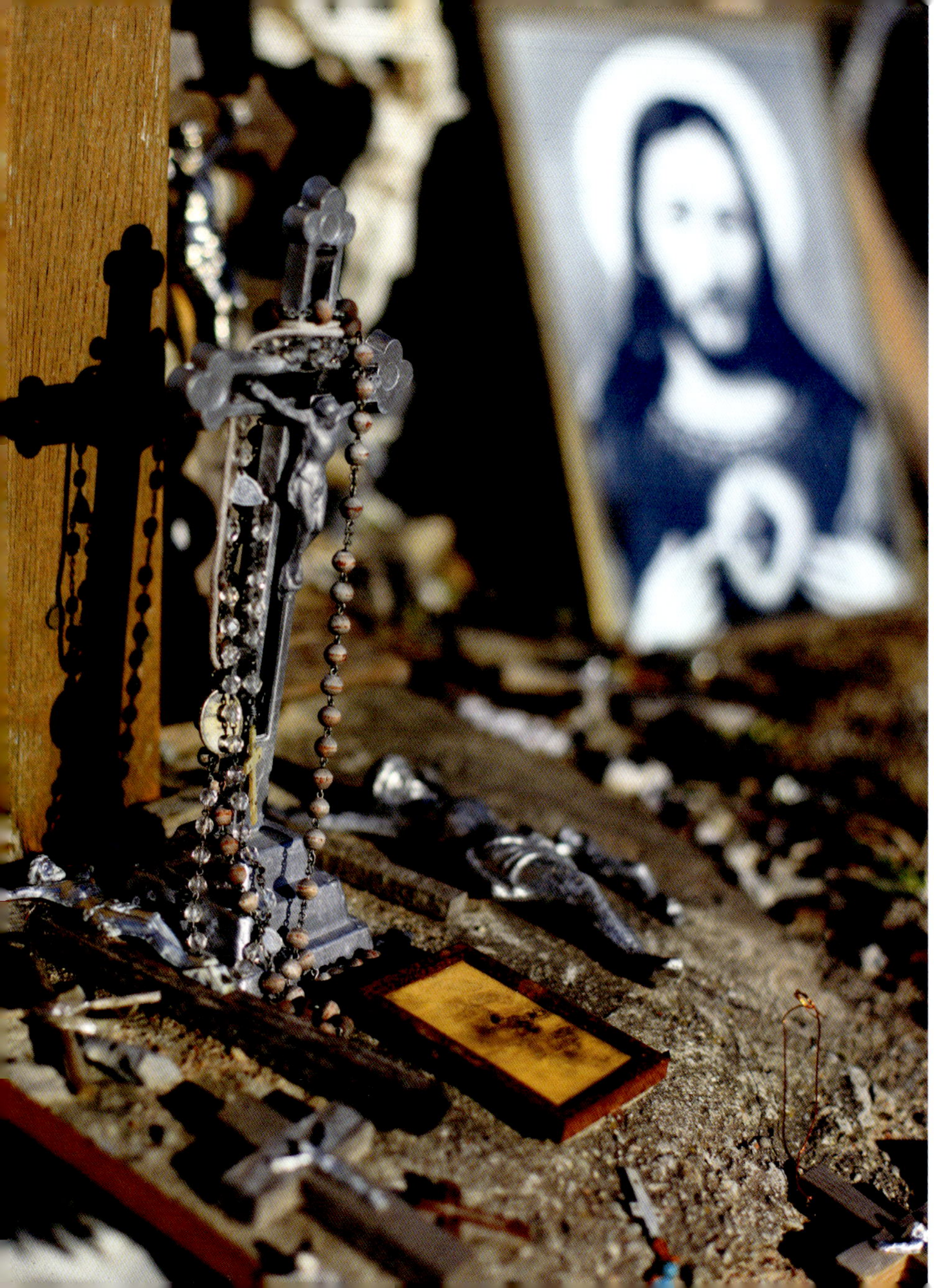

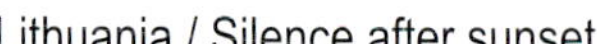

Lithuania / No cross, no crown

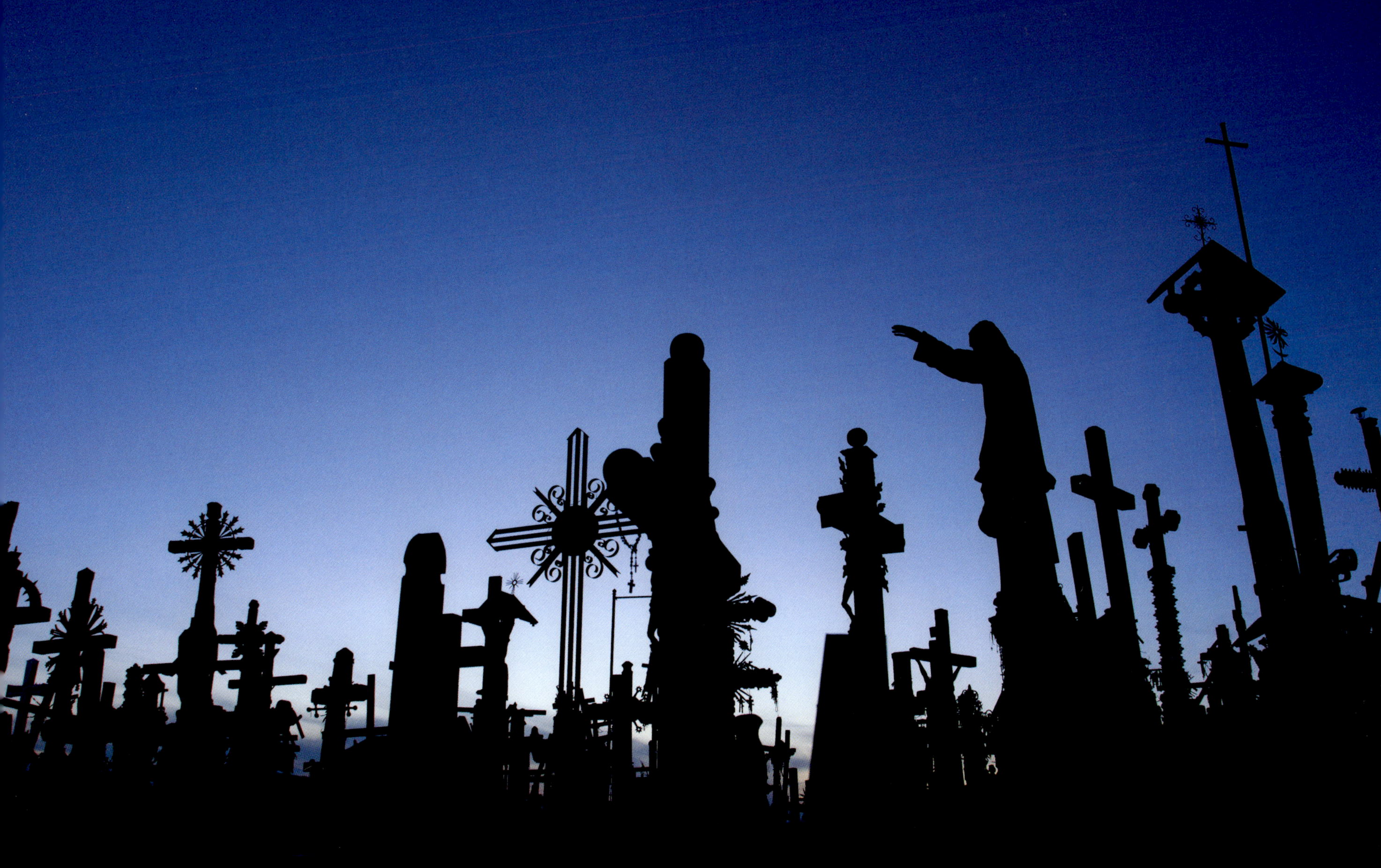

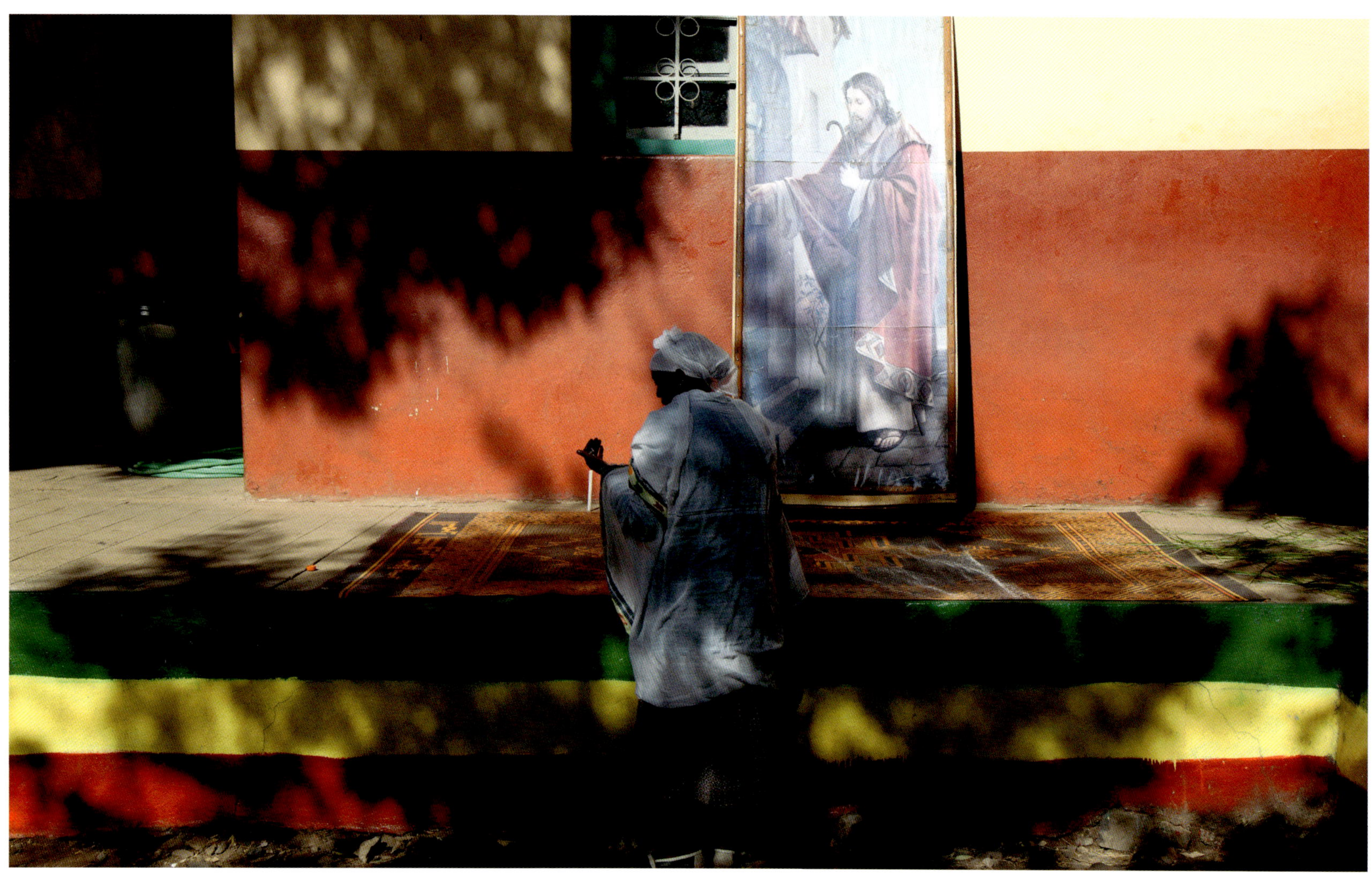

Ethiopia / Ethiopian color

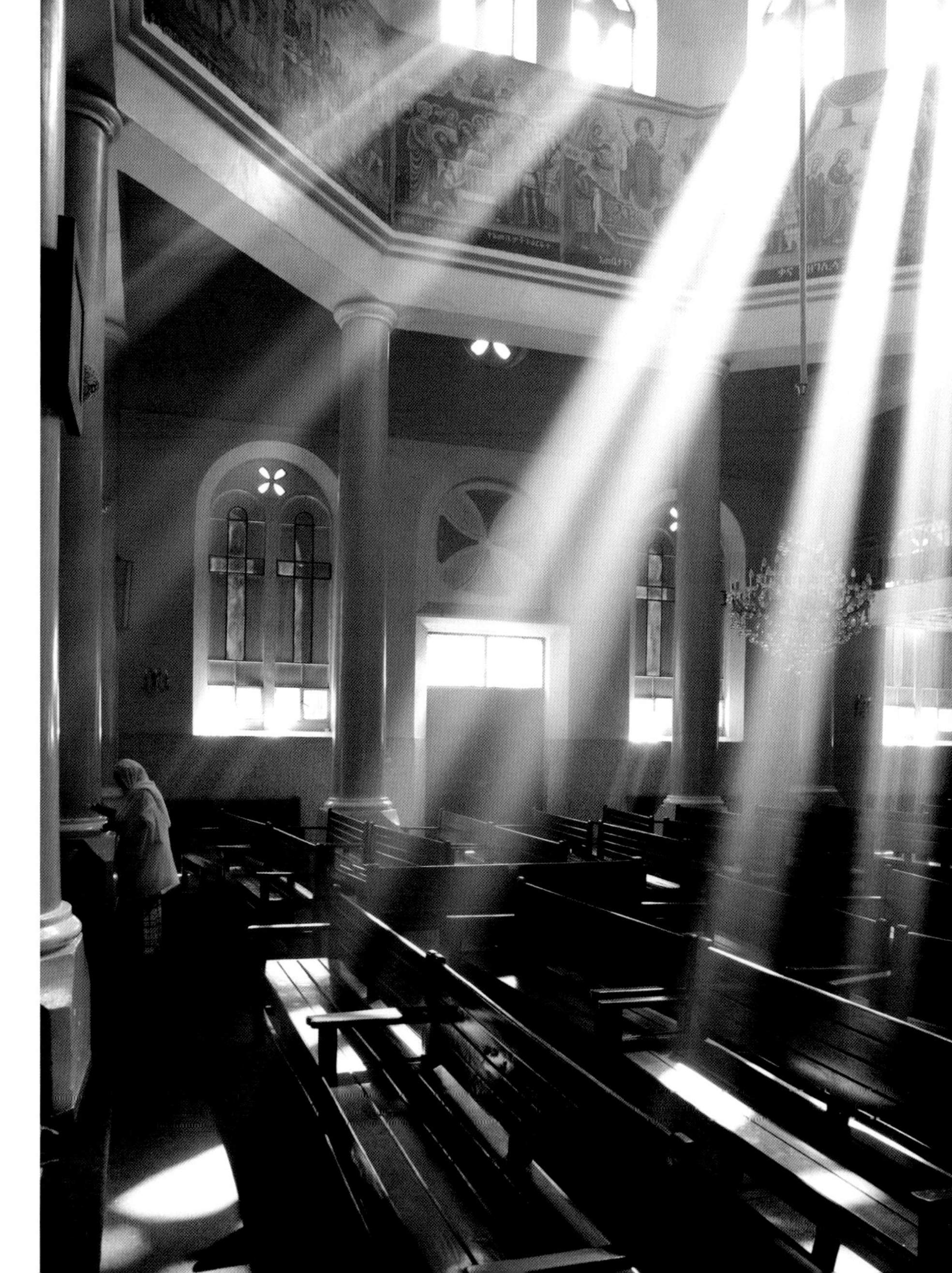

Ethiopia / In the light of holiness...

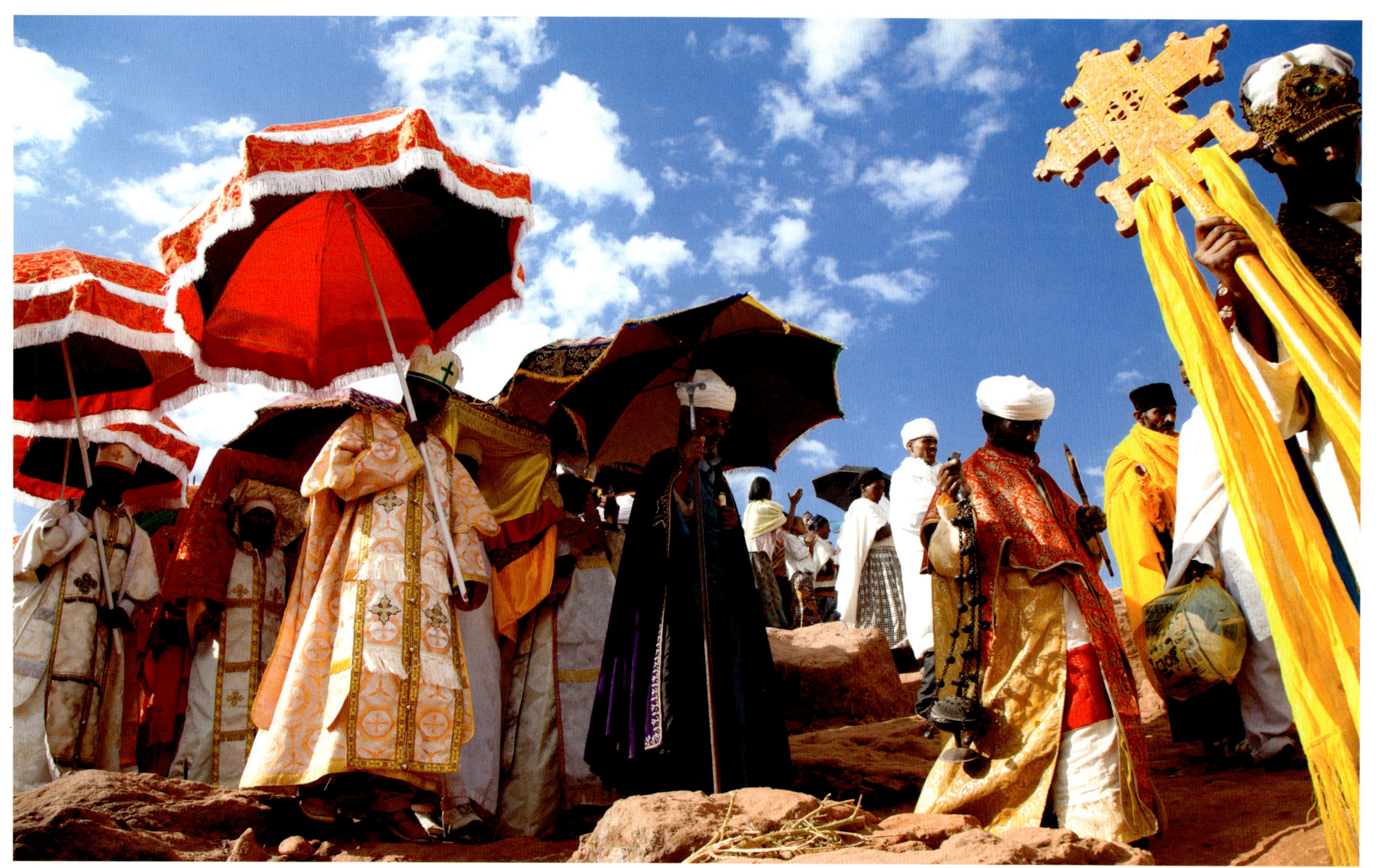

Ethiopia / Divine liturgy

Ethiopia / Sacred dancing

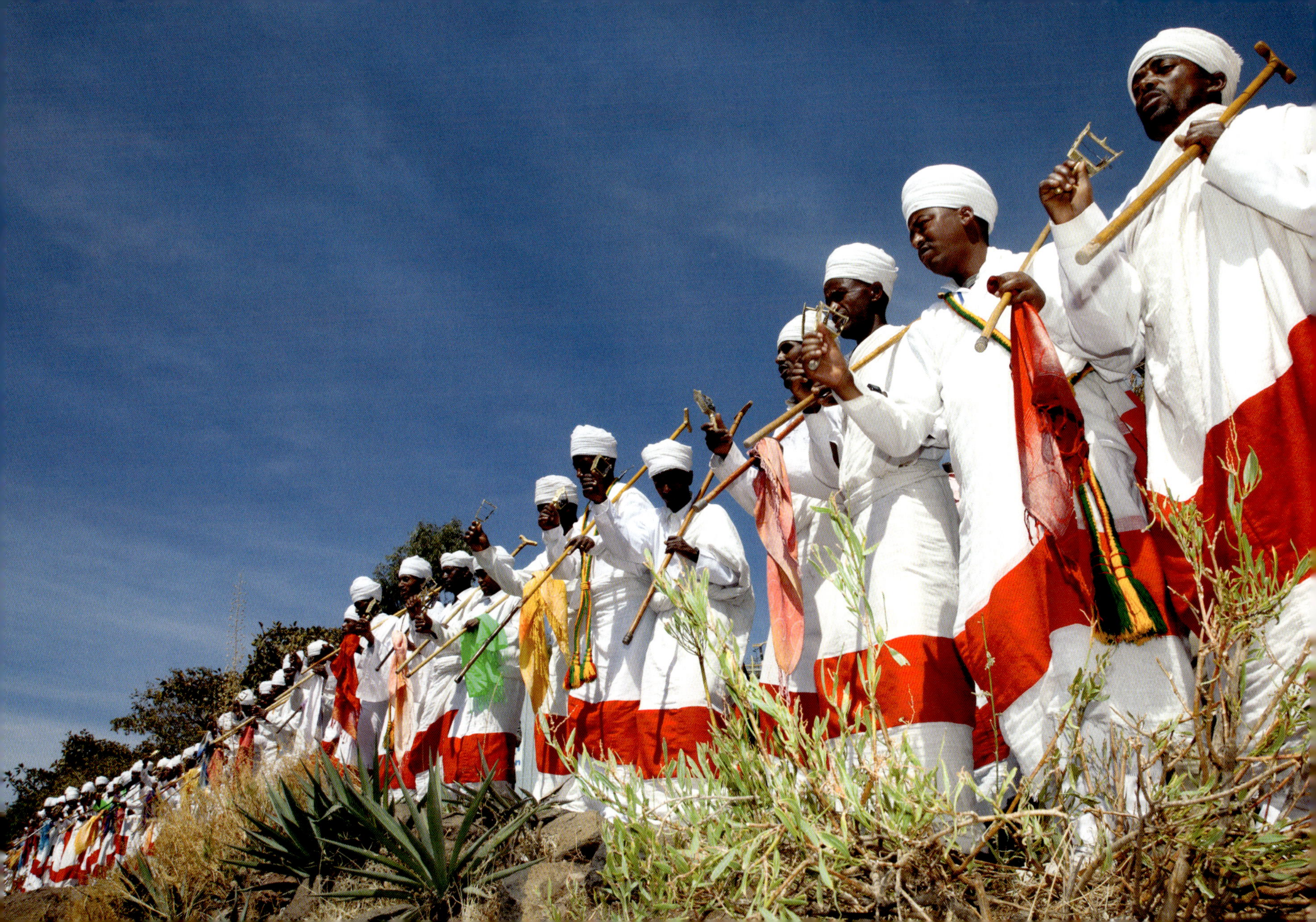

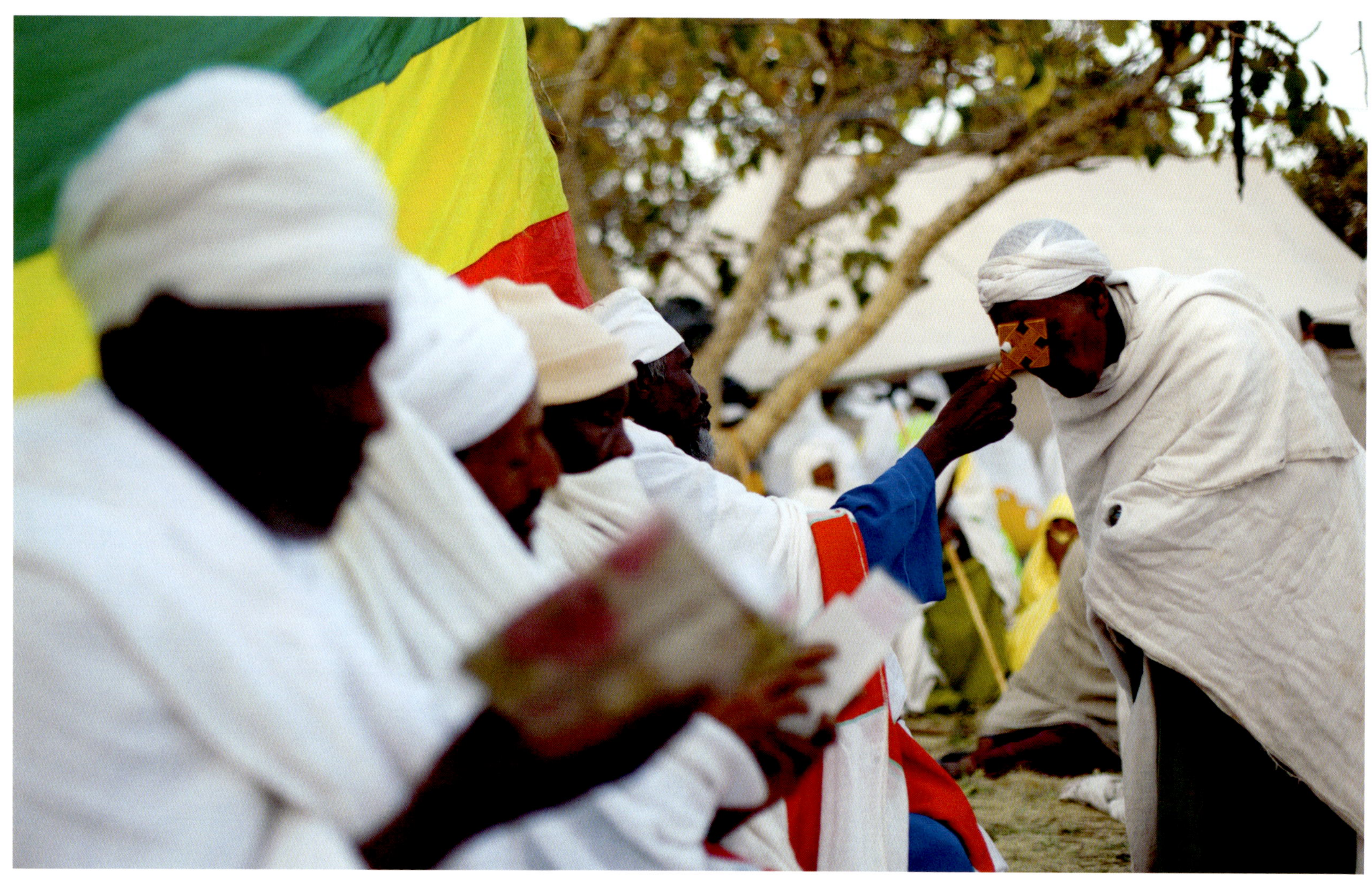

Ethiopia / Divine protection

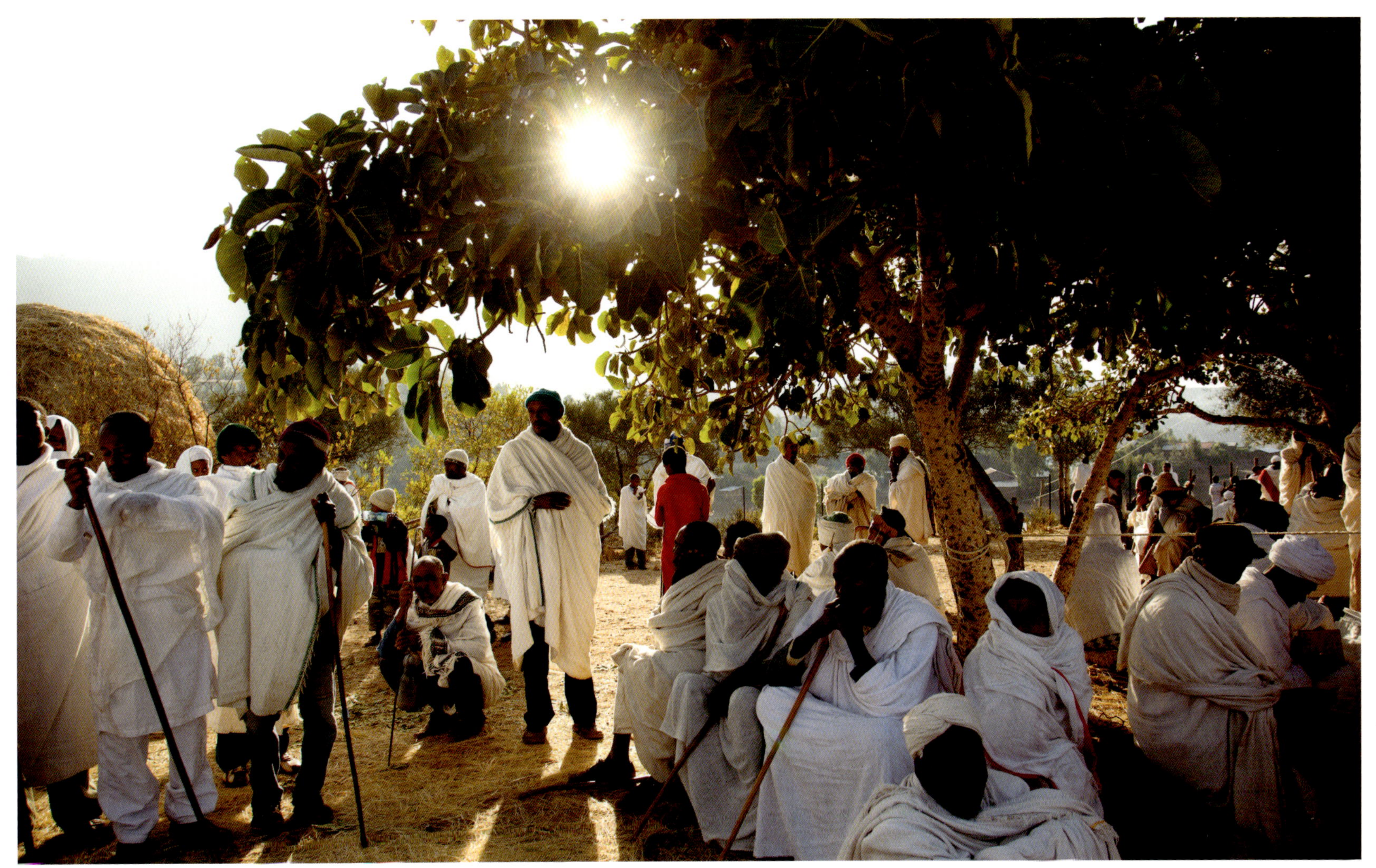

Ethiopia / Various moments

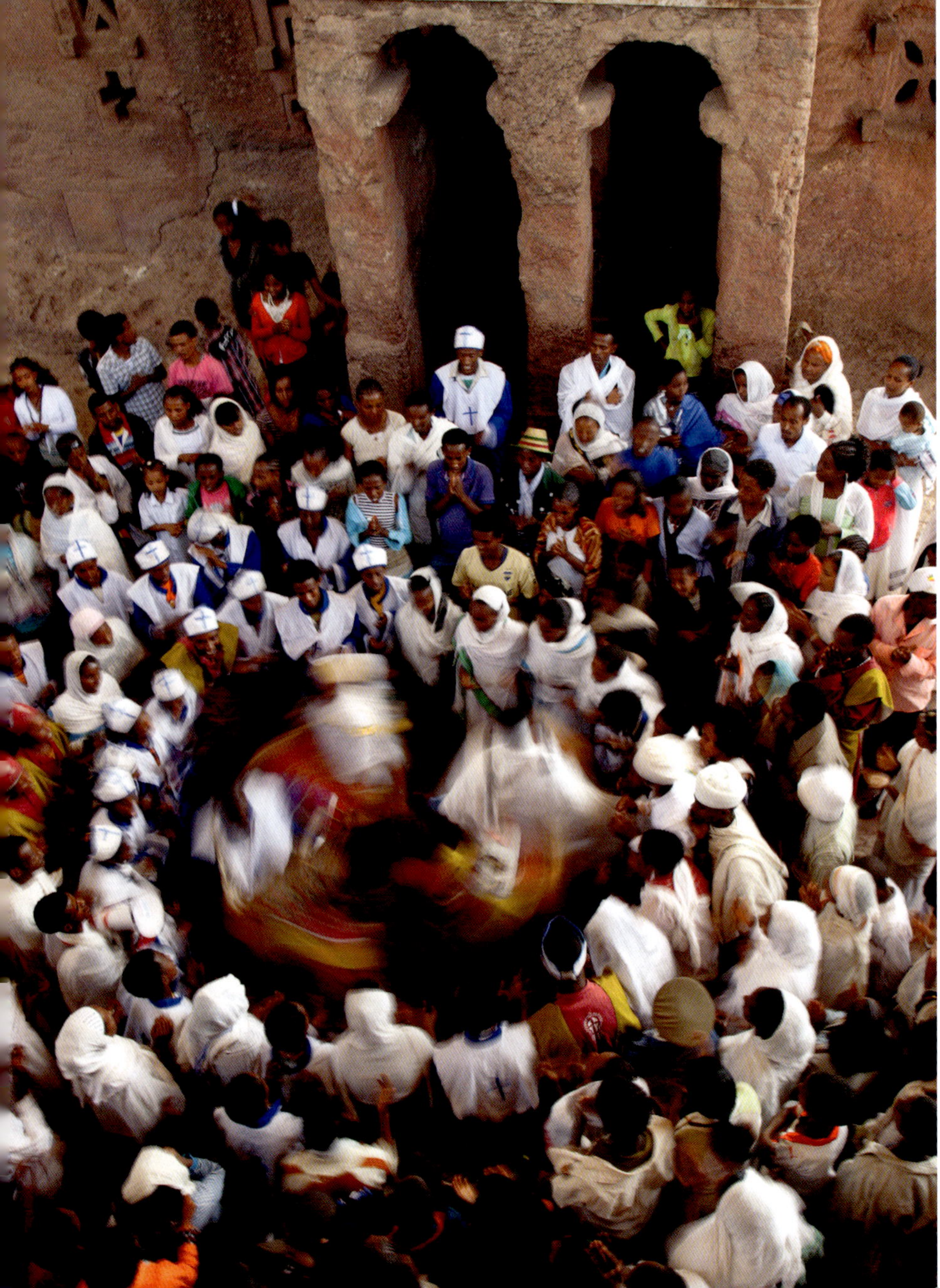

Ethiopia / Time for a celebration

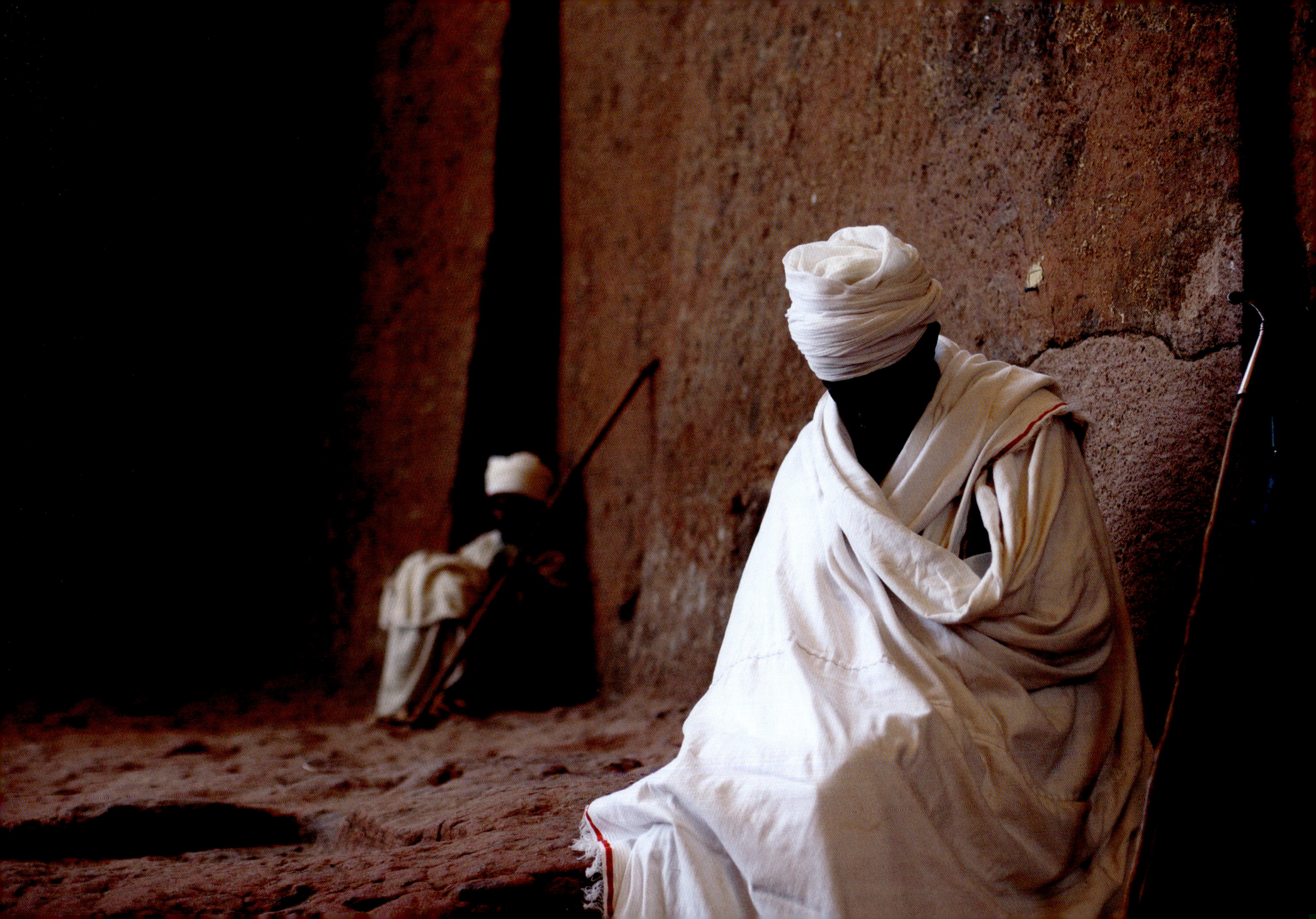

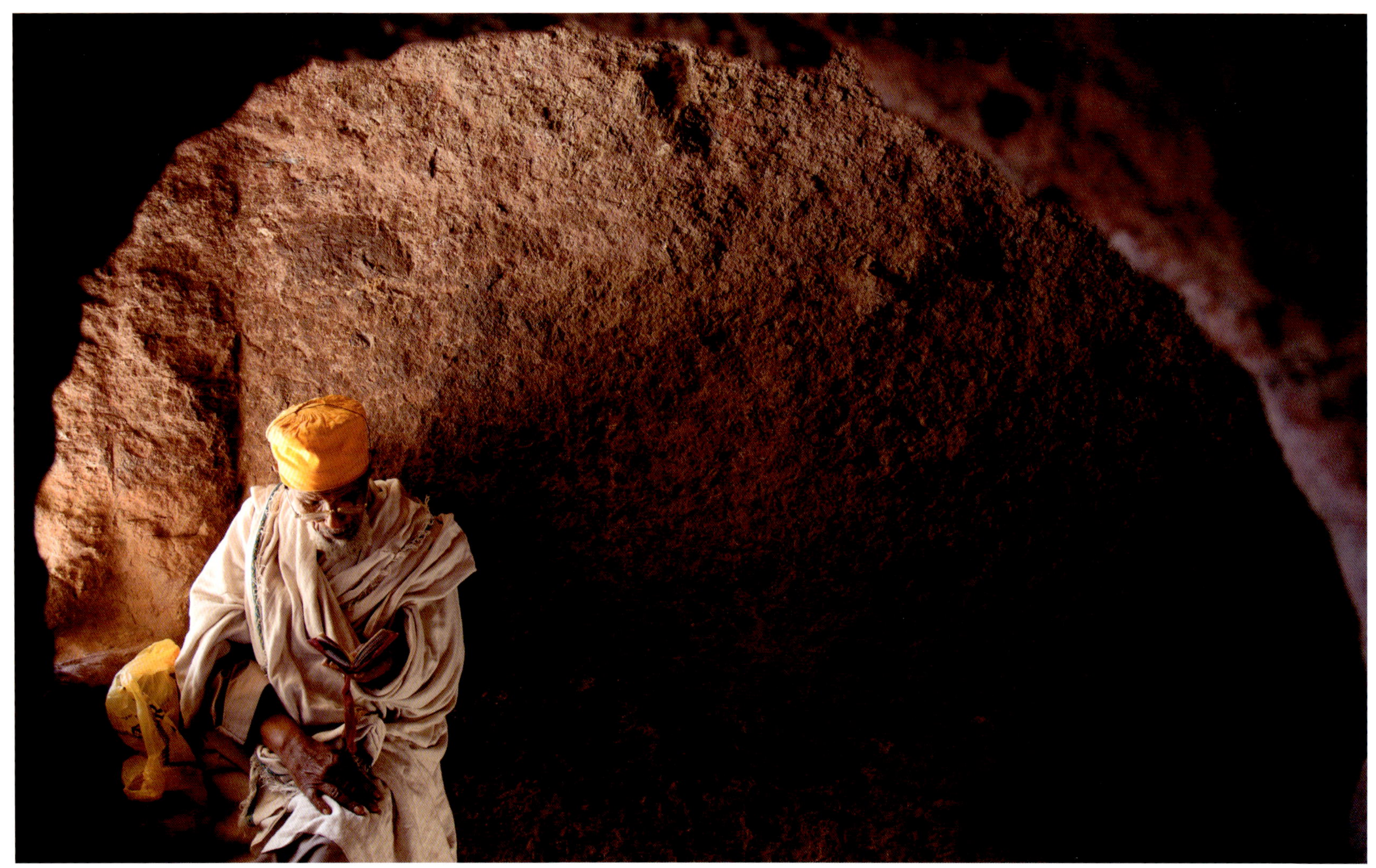

Ethiopia / Holy time

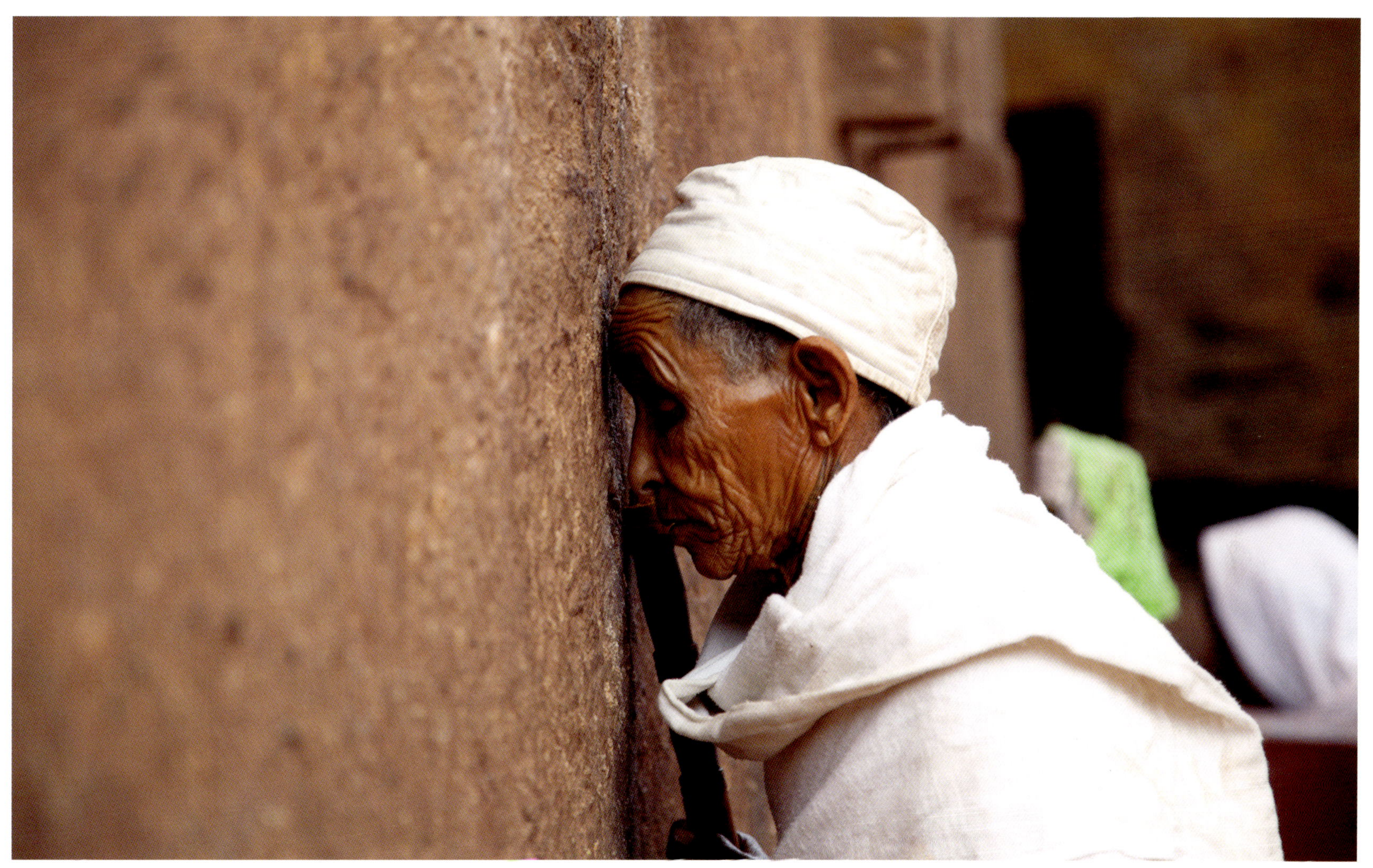

Ethiopia / Devout prayer

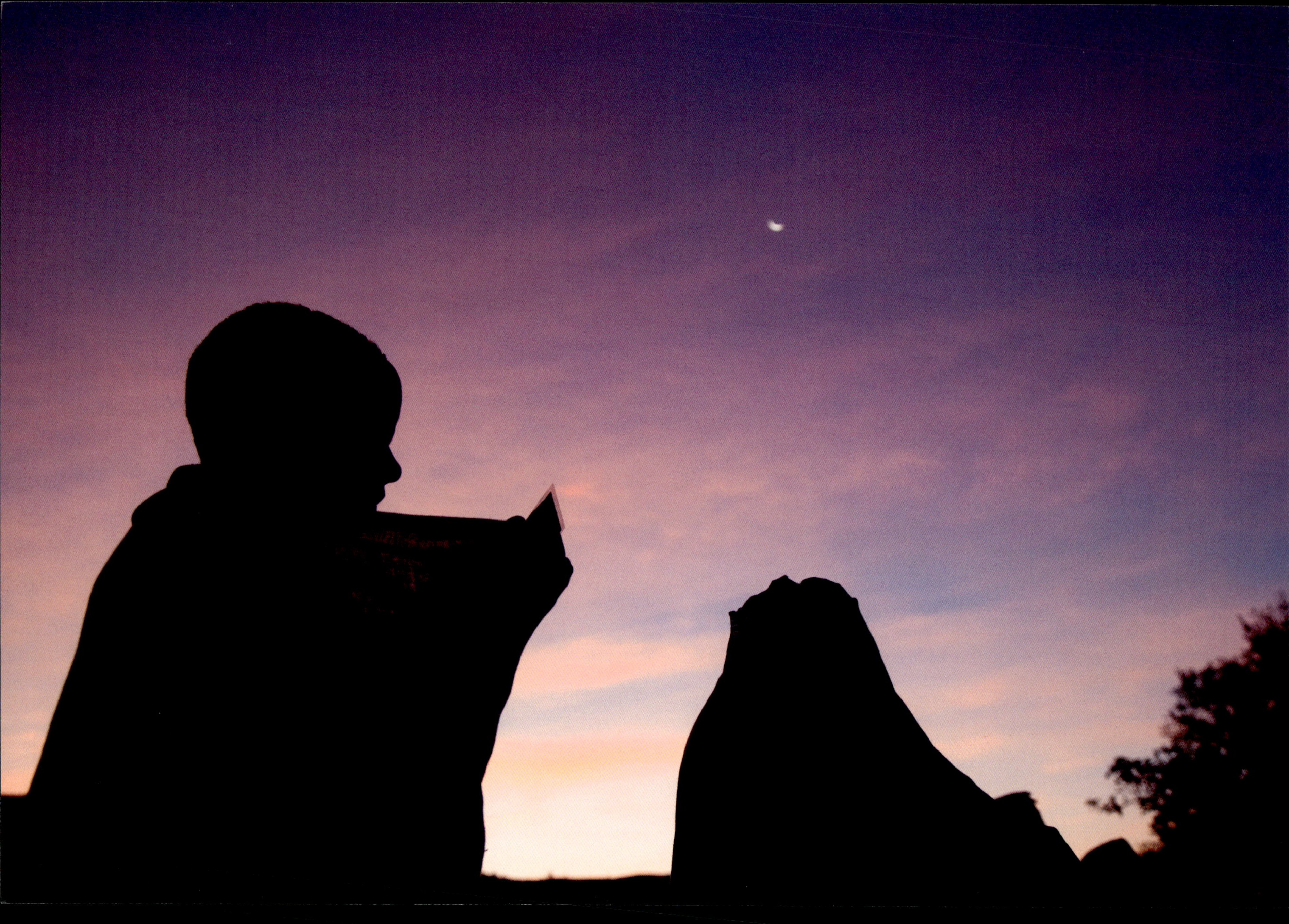

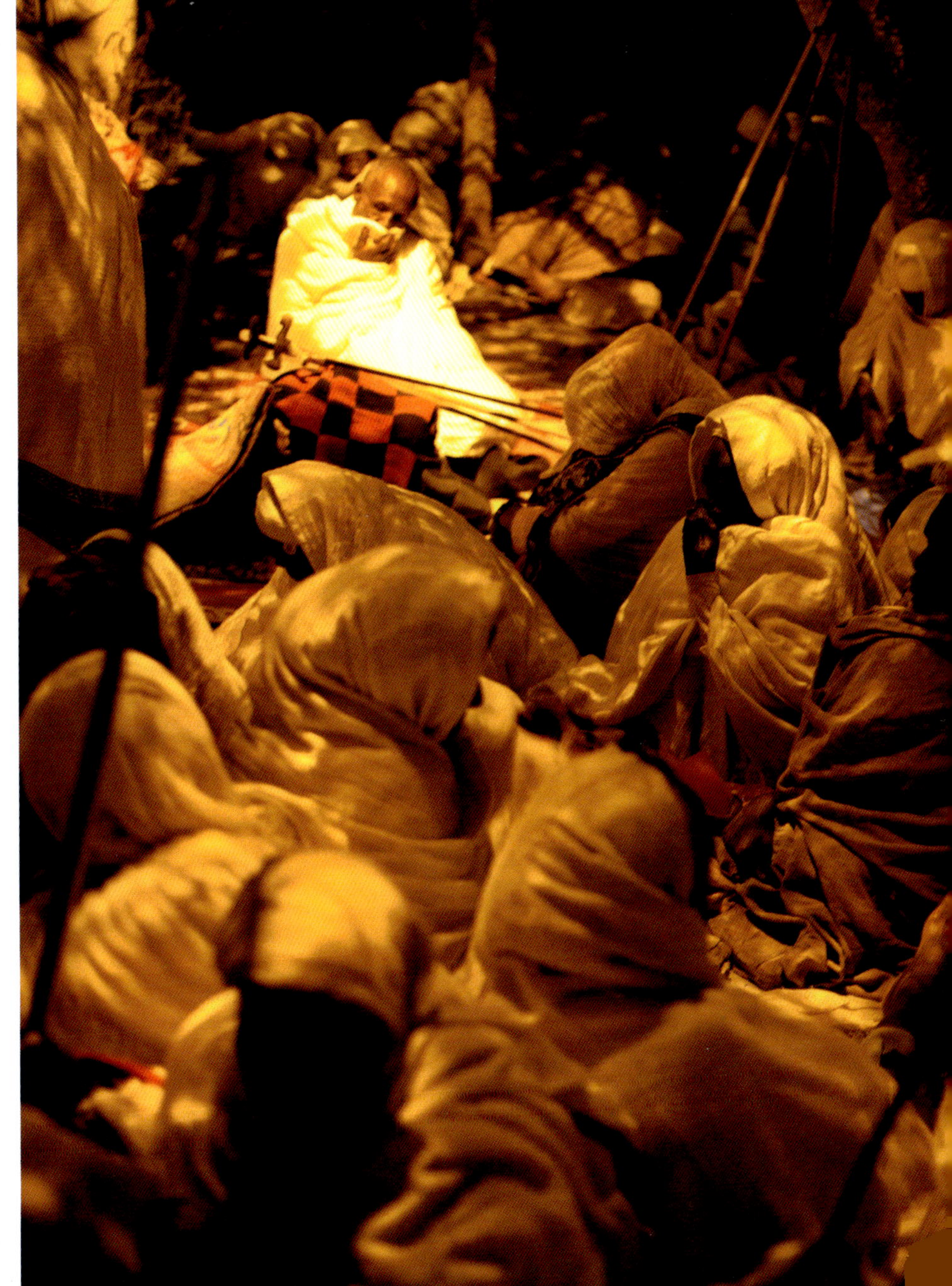

Ethiopia / Waiting for the light of day

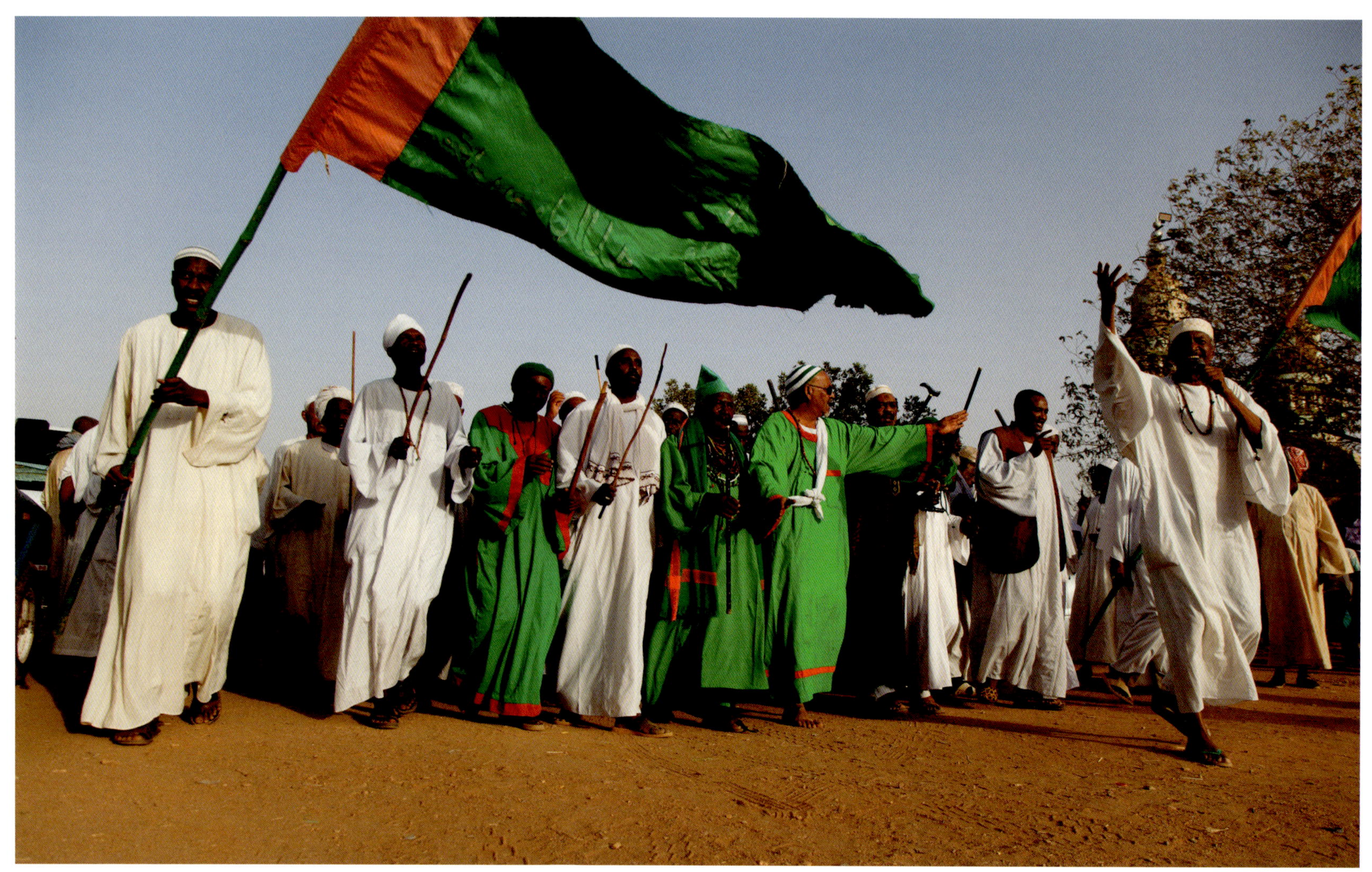

Sudan / Opening ceremony

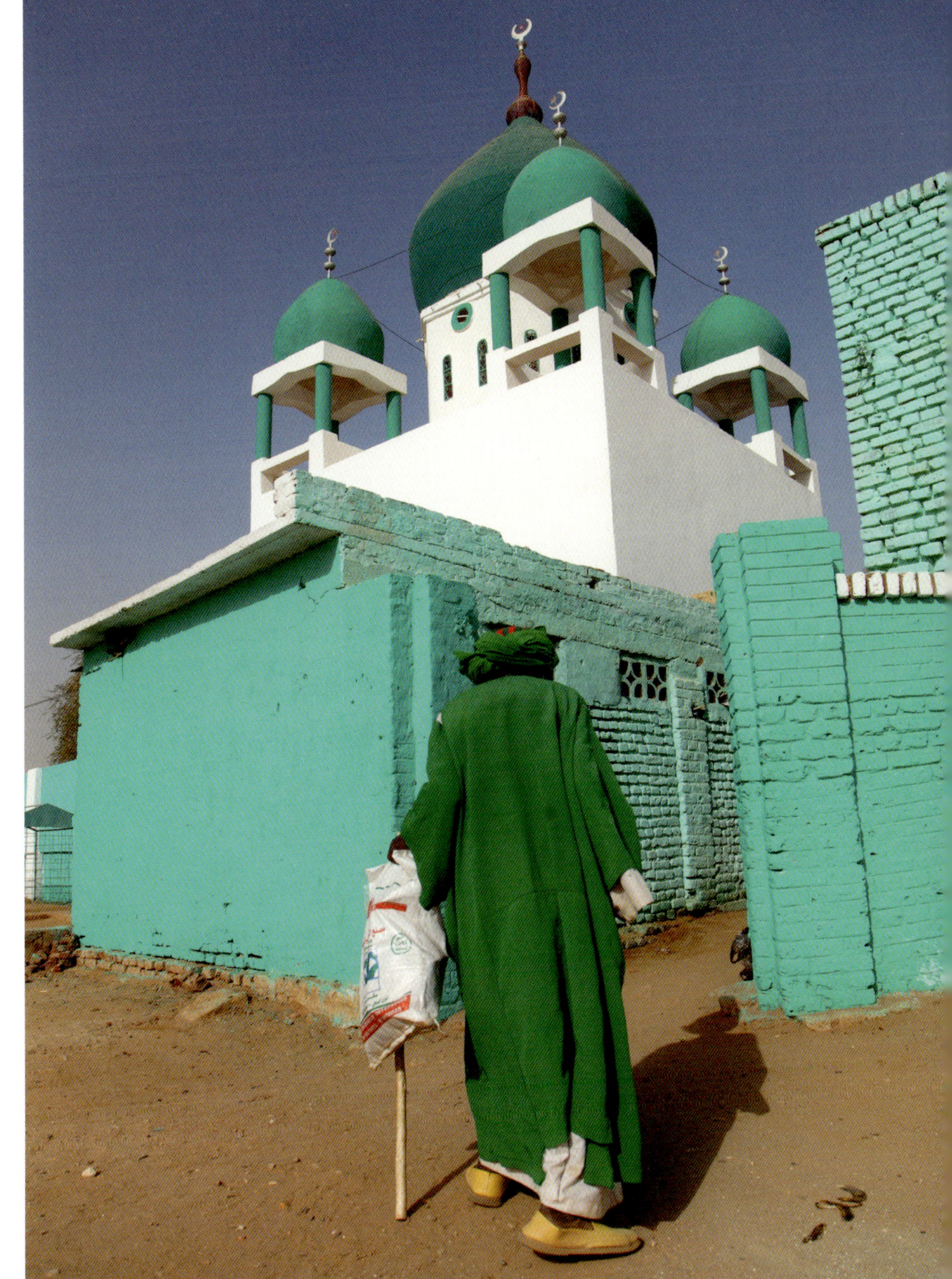

Sudan / Old man visiting mosque

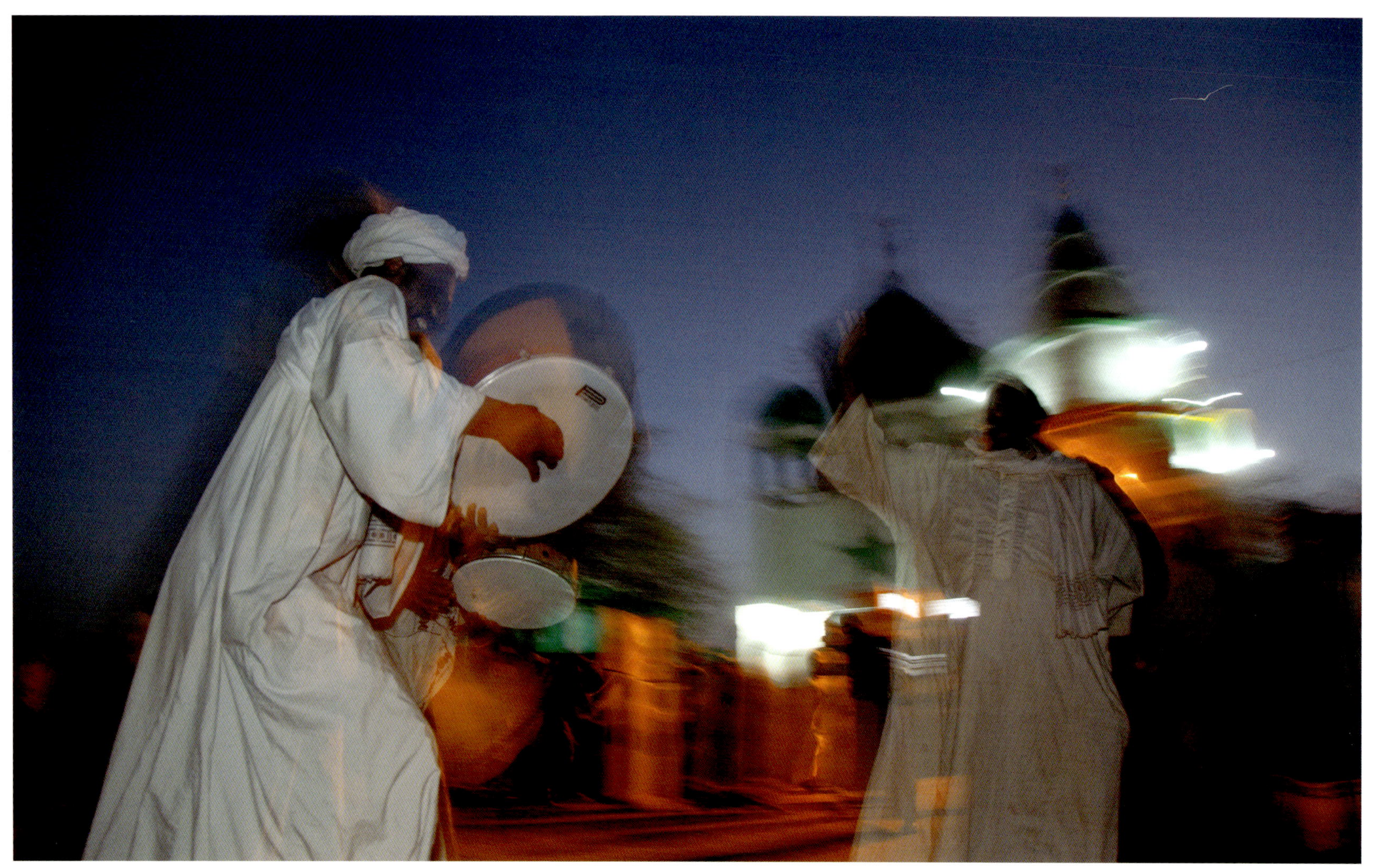

Sudan / Sufi night

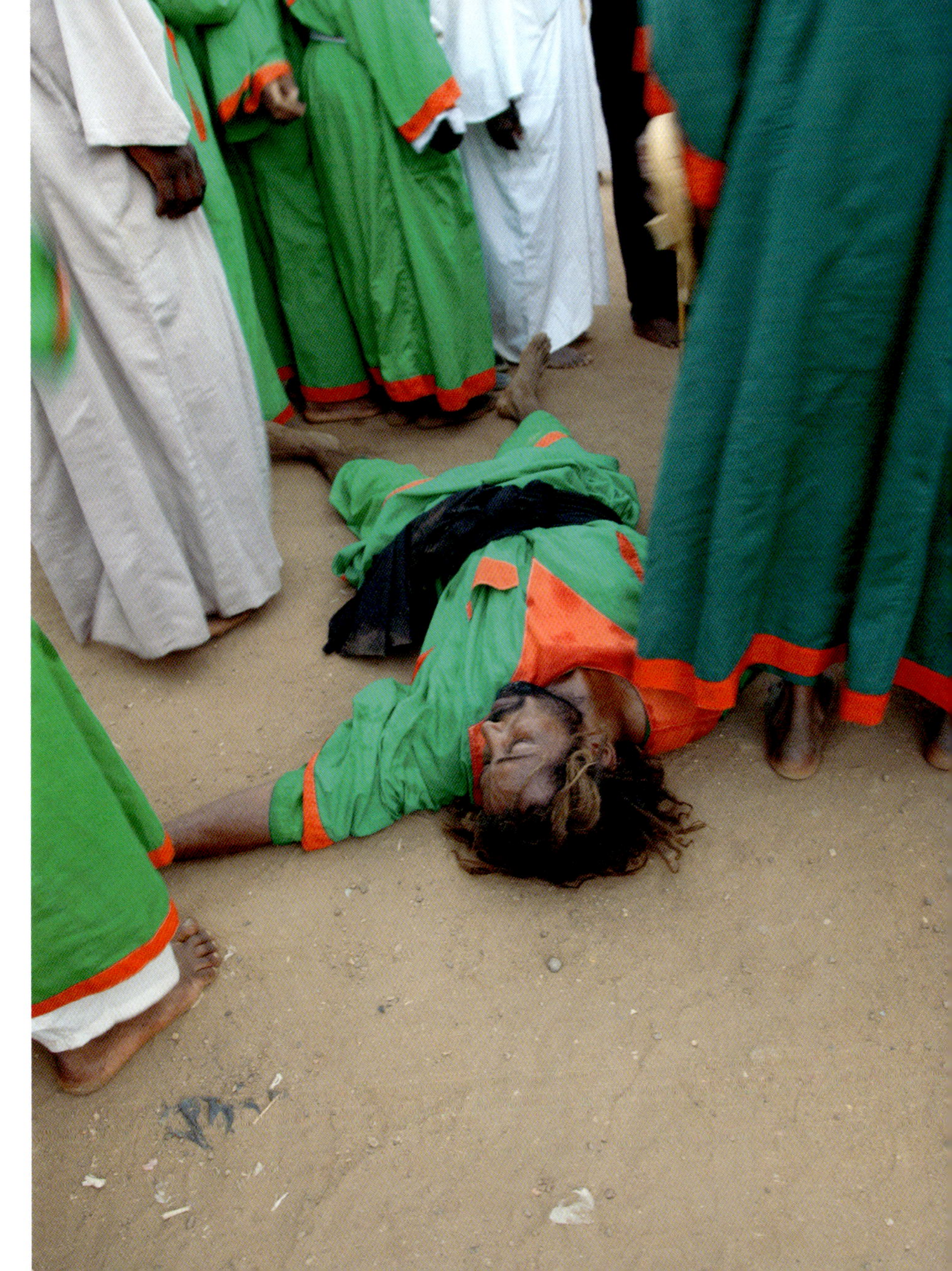

Sudan / Going into a trance

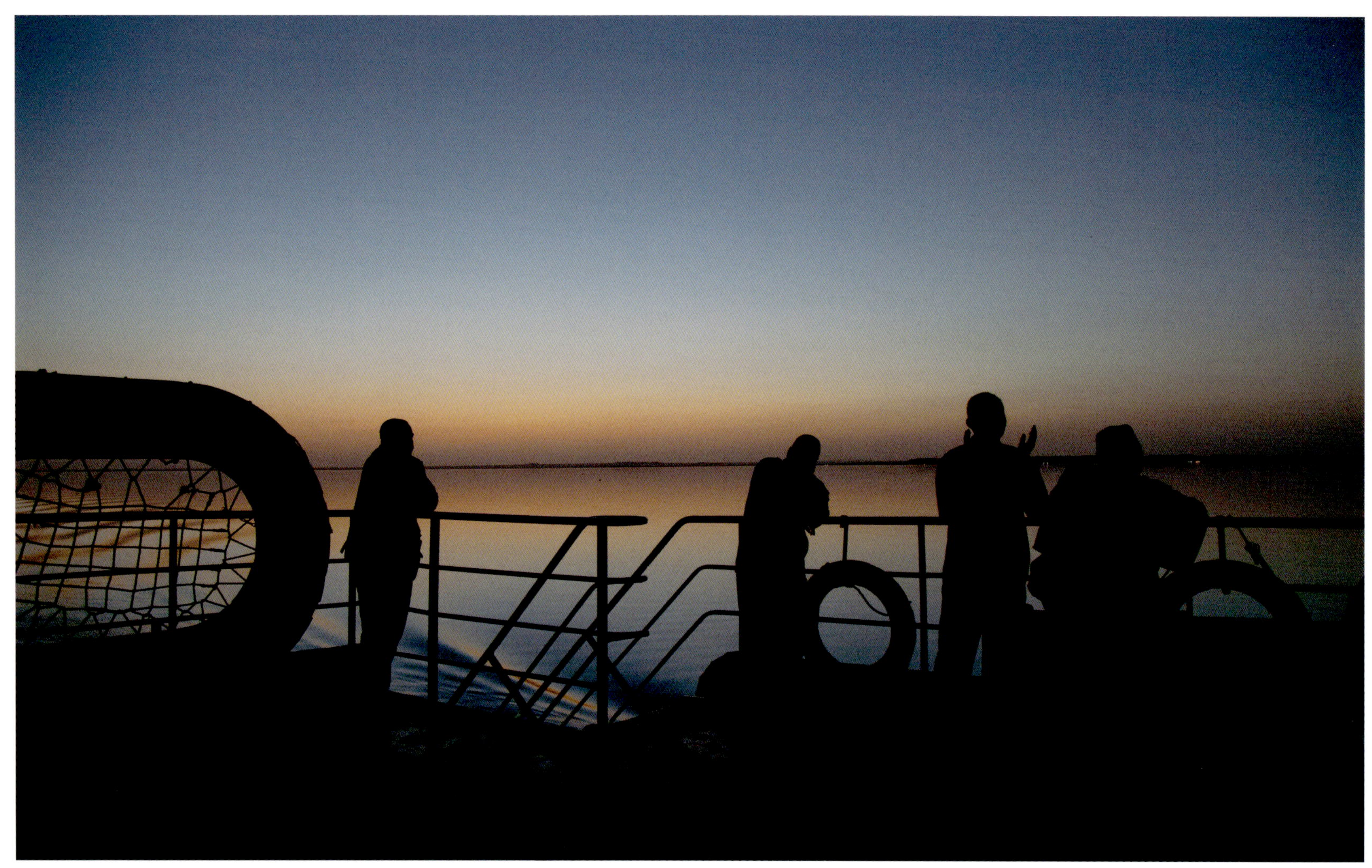

Sudan / The Nile in the twilight

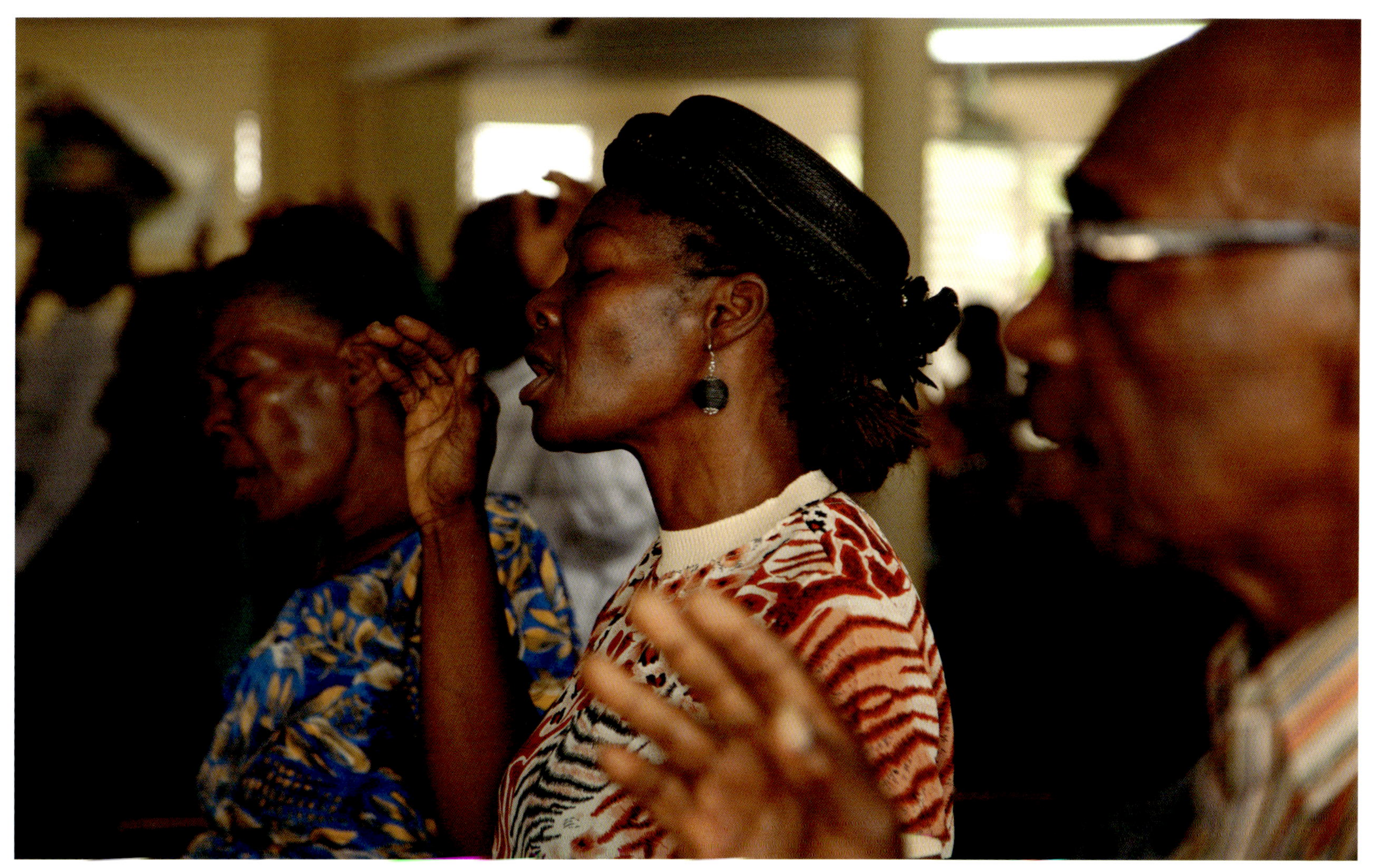

Jamaica / Sunday scene

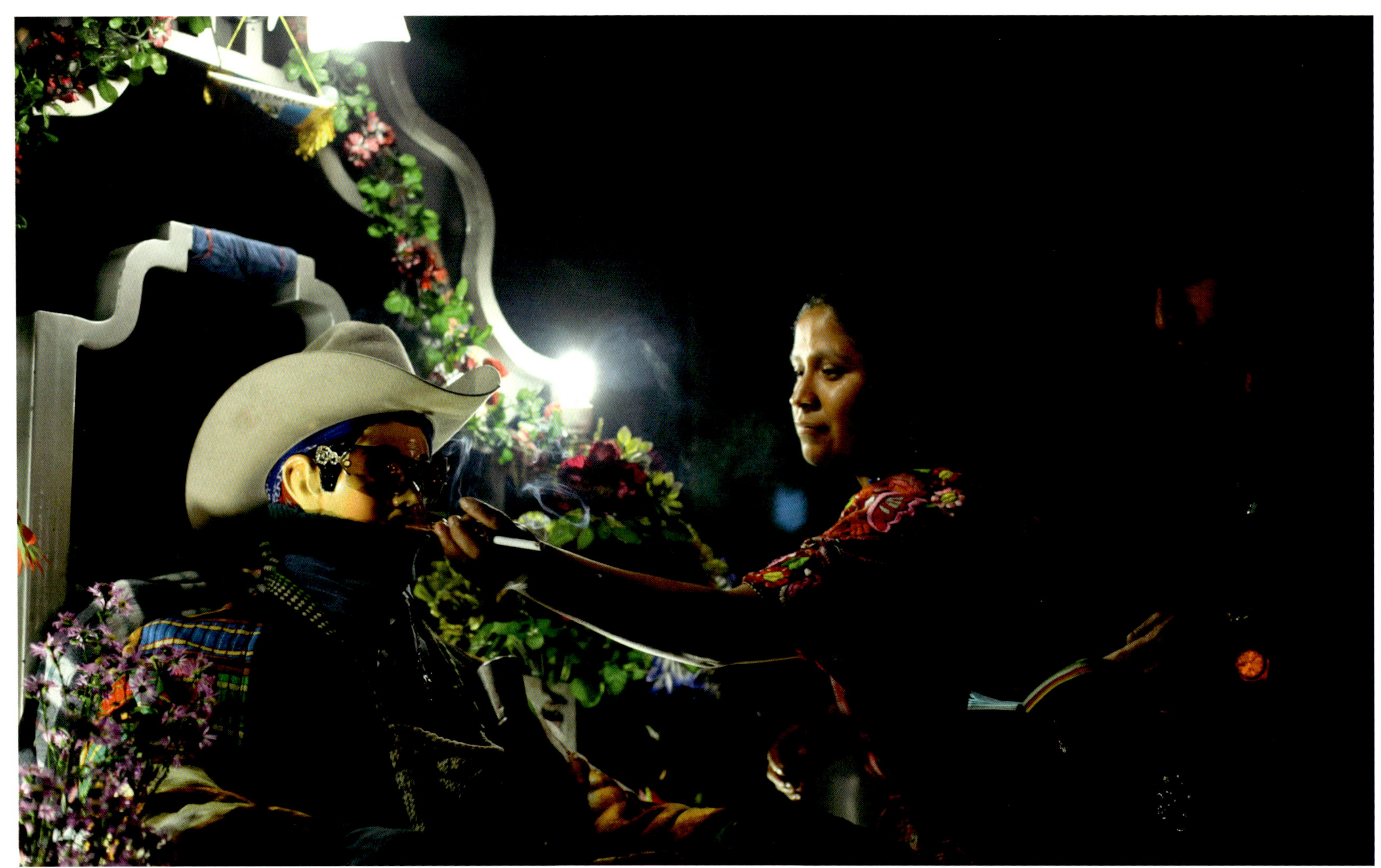

Guatemala / A daily prayer to San Simón

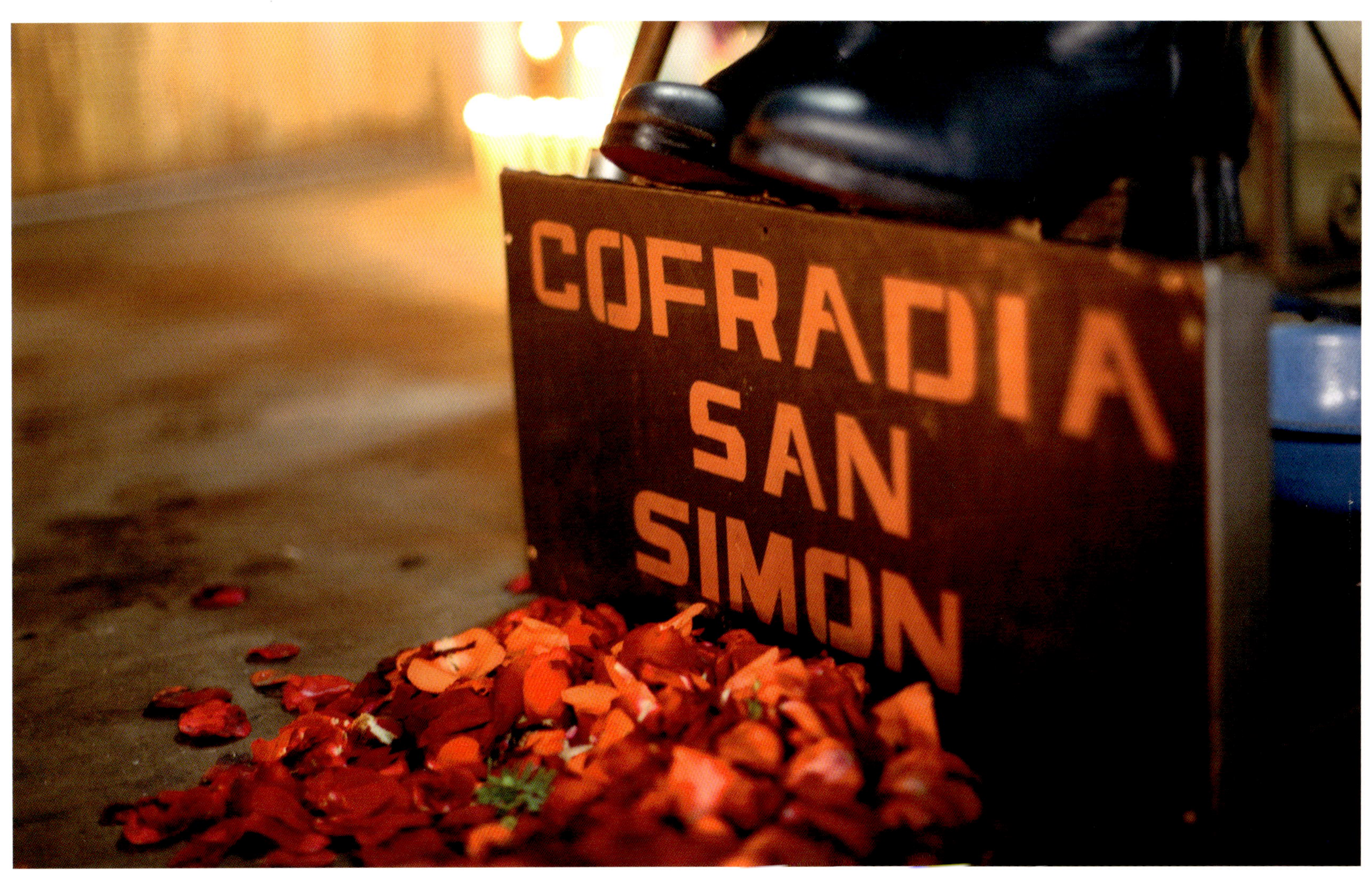

Guatemala / Transition

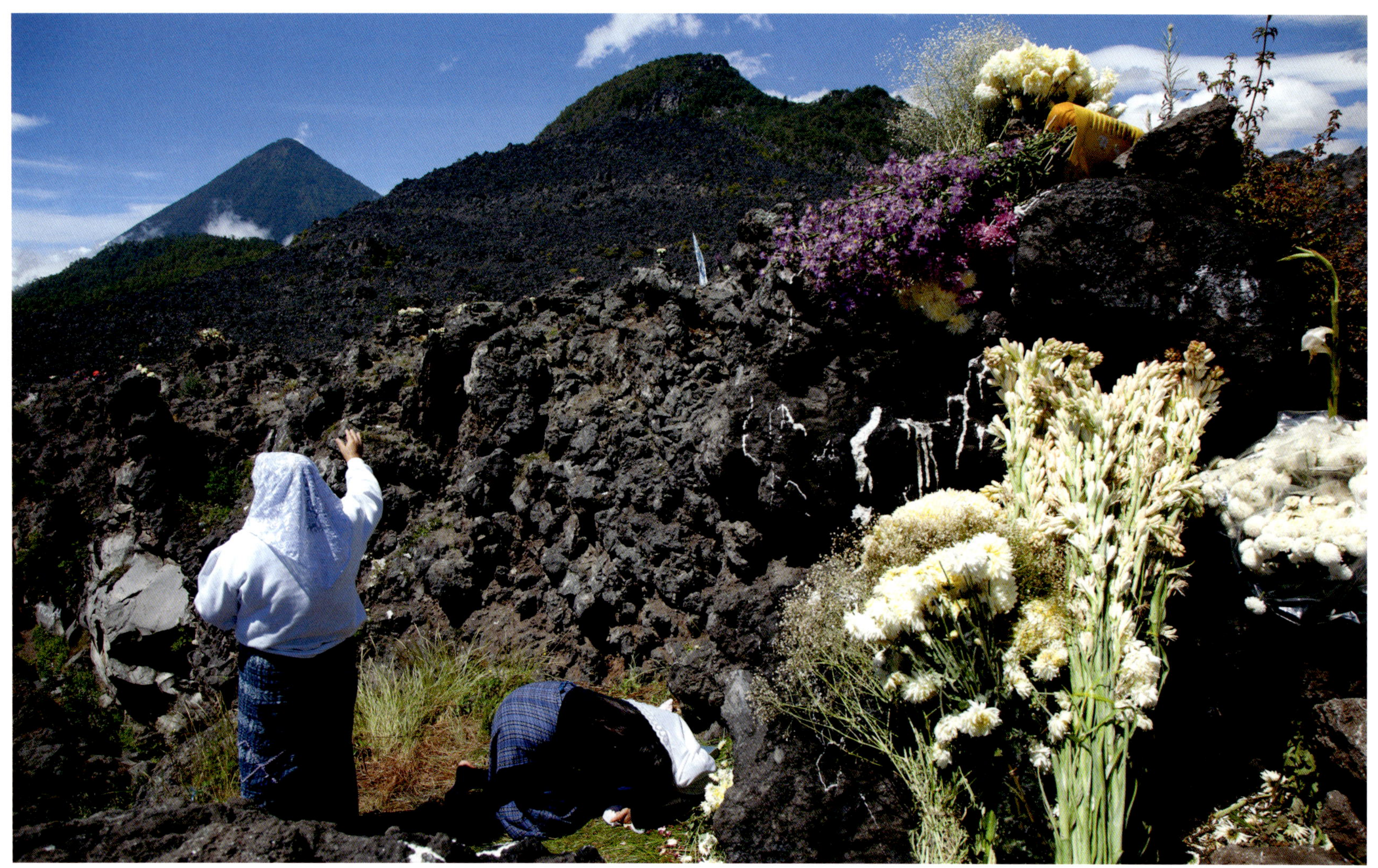

Guatemala / Mother earth

Guatemala / Blessing from nature

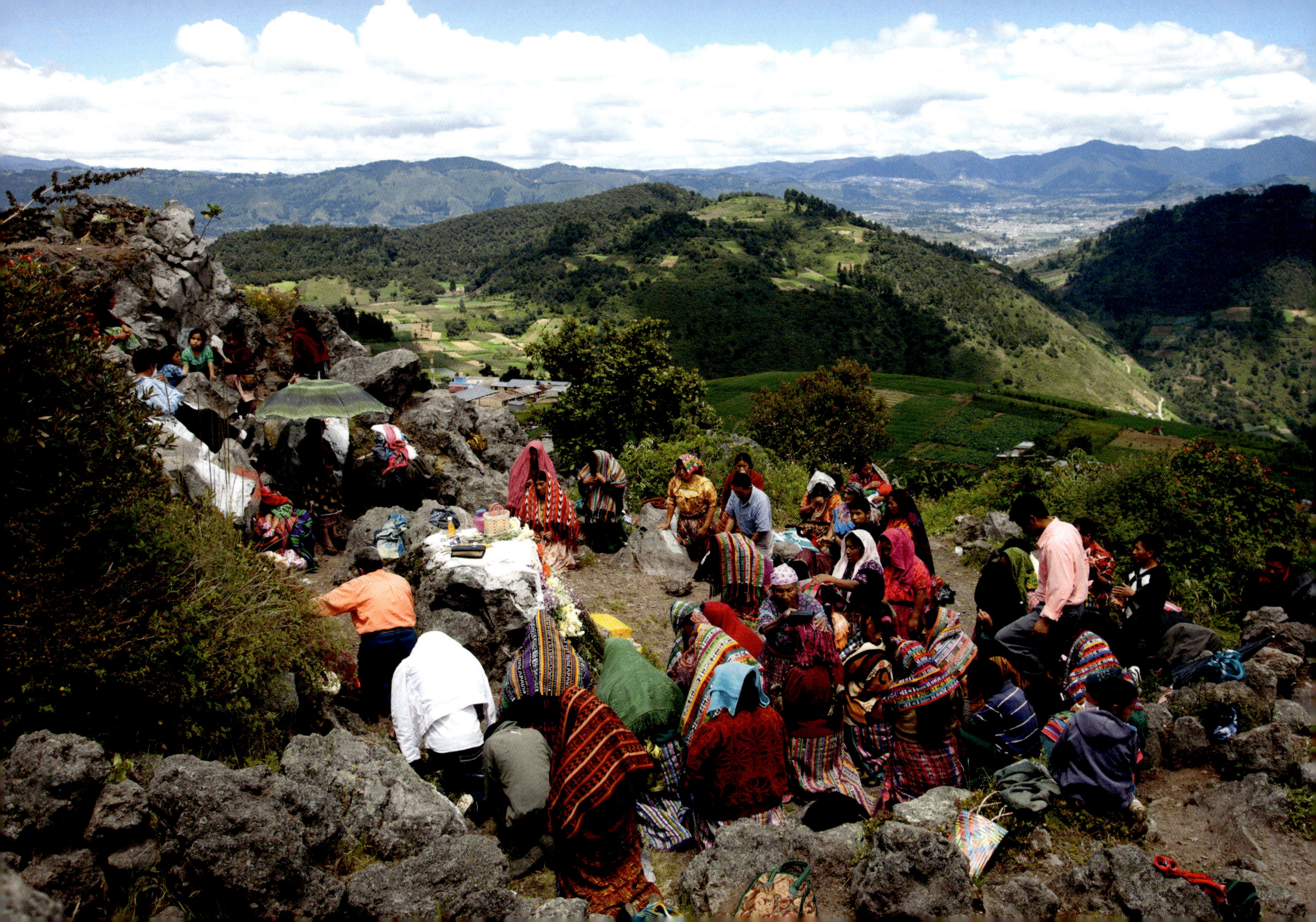

LIST

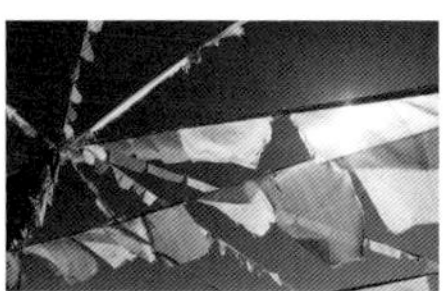

P03

チベット仏教のタルチョと呼ばれる旗。旗には経典や願い事が書かれていて世界中に仏教の教えや、その願いが広まるようにチベットでは至る所でこのカラフルなタルチョが掲げられている。

Tibetan Buddhist tarucho prayer streamers. These colorful tarucho streamers are found all over Tibet, displaying prayerful aspirations and wishes, as they spread the teachings of Buddha to locals and visitors alike.

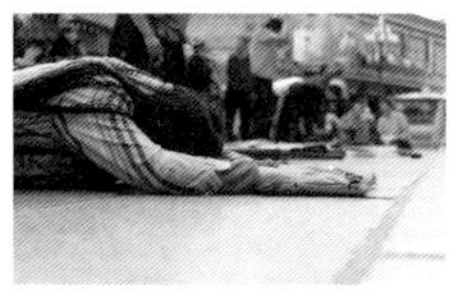

P04

チベットの首都ラサ中心にあるジョカン寺の前で五体投地をする女性。7世紀に建立されたジョカン寺はチベット仏教の総本山とされ、最も重要な寺院でもある。

A woman prostrating herself in the wutitoudi manner in front of Jokhang temple in Lhasa, capital of Tibet. Jokhang temple, erected in the 7th century, is considered to be the head temple of the Tibetan sect of Buddhism and is its most important holy place.

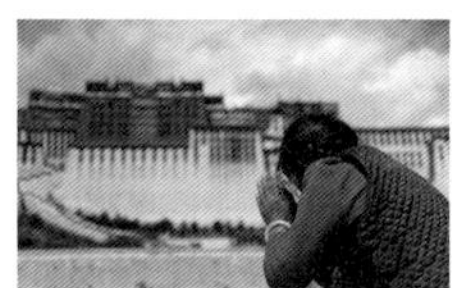

P05

ラサにあるポタラ宮殿の前で祈る仏教徒。ポタラ宮殿もチベット人にとって重要な建造物の一つ。周りには常に中国警察が警備をしている。

Buddhists praying in front of the Potala Palace in Lhasa. The Potala Palace is of key significance for Tibetans. Chinese police patrols maintain a permanent presence at this site.

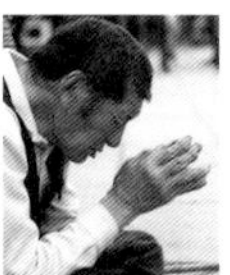

P06

同じくジョカン寺の前で熱心に祈りを捧げる男性。チベット人にとってジョカン寺に訪れることは最高の喜びでもある。多くの人がチベット各地から五体投地でこの場所を目指す。

Man deep in prayer at Jokhang temple. A visit to this temple is a joyous occasion for Tibetans. When prostrating themselves in prayer, many Tibetans all over the country will align their bodies in the general direction of Jokhang temple.

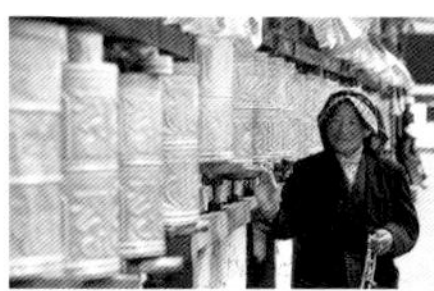

P07

マニ車と呼ばれるチベット仏教には欠かせない道具。写真の様に壁に掛かっているのと、携帯出来る手持ち用のがある。一周回す度に一回経典を読んだ事になる。

The spinning mani prayer wheel is an indispensable device in Tibetan Buddhism. Some are to be found hanging on walls as if they were a picture. Others are carried in the hand and each revolution of the wheel counts as one mantra.

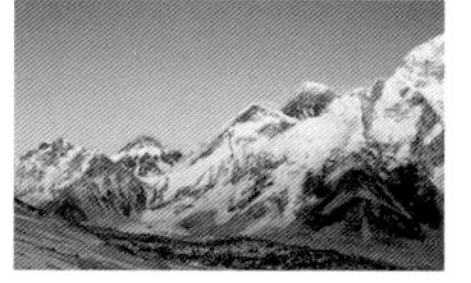

P08

ネパールにある聖山マチャプチャレ山。前にある槍はヒンドゥー教の神様の一人シヴァ神が持つ三叉の槍。

Mount Machapuchare sacred peak in Nepal. The three-pronged spear in front of the mountain represents that of the Hindu god, Shiva the Destroyer.

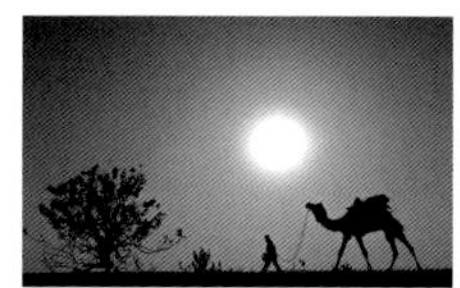

P09

仏陀が生まれた町ルンビニの夜明け。薄ら見える建物は仏教の広まっている国々によって建設された寺院や仏塔。

Daybreak over the town of Rumbini, the Buddha's birthplace. A temple and the pagoda are visible, built by the peoples to whom Buddhism spread.

P10

仏陀が生まれたとされている場所マーヤー夫人堂の前で祈る尼僧達。

Nuns praying in front of Maya Devi temple, the site of the Buddha's birth.

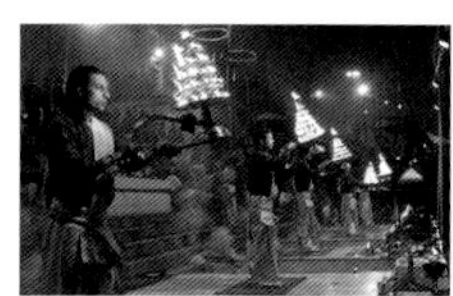

P11

世界の屋根であるエヴェレストが夕日に染まった瞬間。ネパールの人達は聖なる山として崇めている。

The moment that Mt. Everest, the roof of the world, is touched by the sunset. The people of Nepal revere it as a sacred mountain.

P13

インドにある砂漠の町ジャイサルメール。灼熱の砂漠では毎日ノマド達がラクダと共に生活をしている。

The desert town of Jaisalmer in India. Everyday life with nomadic camels in the scorching sands.

P14

ヴァラナシを流れるガンジス川沿いで毎日行われるプジャーというヒンドゥー教の儀式。

The Hindu ritual of Puja which is performed daily in the river Ganges as it flows past the city of Varanasi.

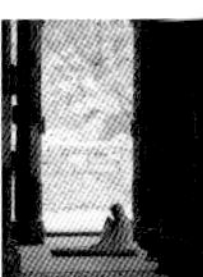

P15 ——————

インドでイスラム教徒が多く住む町アジメールで祈りを捧げる信者。

Worshippers gather to pray at Ajmer, an Indian town with many Muslims.

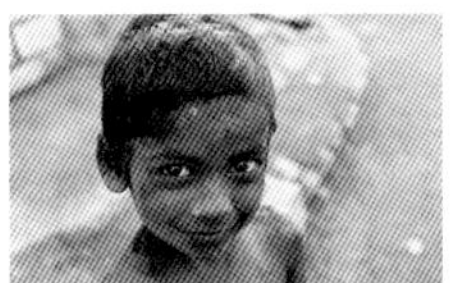

P16 ——————

インドでもっともカラフルで賑やかなお祭りホーリー祭 (Holi)。豊作祈願や悪霊退治の目的で色粉を塗り合い、掛け合ってお祝いする。期間中は各地で繰り広げられる。

The Holi festival in India is a most colorful and lively celebration. The many powder colorings are used to ward off evil spirits and to pray for and celebrate a bounteous harvest. This festival is held all over India during These are common features of festivals all over India during this time.

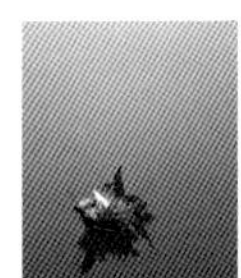

P17 ——————

ヒンドゥー教の儀式プジャーではガンジス川へそれぞれの想いや祈りを込めて献花しロウソクを灯す。

In the Hindu Puja ceremony, flowers and sparkling candles accompany hopes and prayers along the Ganges.

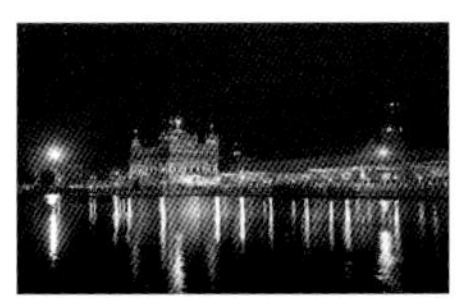

P18 ——————

シク教の総本山インドのアムリトサルにあるゴールデンテンプル。寺院の周りは池になっていてシク教徒達は沐浴をして身を清める。ここでは毎日たくさんの信者が訪れ、祈りが捧げられている。

The Golden Temple of Amritsar is the holiest shrine of Sikhism. Those of the Sikh faith wash their feet in a pool to purify themselves. Each day brings a multitude of devotees.

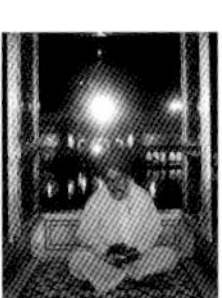

P19 ——————

ゴールデンテンプル内で経典を読むシク教徒。シク教では偶像崇拝を禁止しているため神様はいない。寺院の中央には聖典であるグランド・サーヒブが安置されている。

Sikh scripture reading in the Golden Temple. The precepts of Sri Guru Granth Sahib are enshrined in the center of the temple. Idolatry is forbidden in Sikhism.

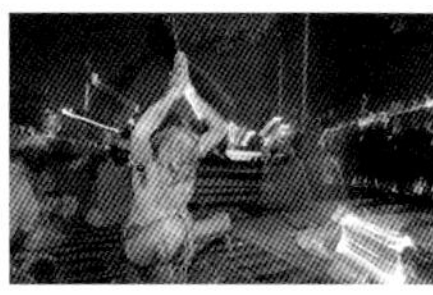

P20 ——————

ガンジス川畔で焚き火の前で祈りを捧げるサドゥー（ヒンドゥー教の修行僧）ヒンドゥー教徒にとって一部のサドゥーは神の化身として扱われる。

A Sadhu, or Hindu monk, praying in front of a fire on the banks of the Ganges. Some Sadhus are venerated as manifestations of gods by Hindus.

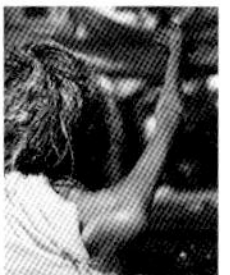

P21 ——————

１３年間右手を挙げ続ける修行を行う苦行者の背中。クンブメーラという世界最大級のお祭りにて。このお祭りでは期間中３０００万人以上の人々が訪れるという。

Strict ascetic discipline leads a follower to keep their right hand raised for 13 years. At the world's largest festival in Kunbumera, visitors number in excess of 30 million.

P22,23 ——————

ミャンマーのバガン。世界三大仏教遺跡でもあるこの街には広大な森に無数のパゴダ（仏塔）が建ち並び、その数は３０００以上にも及ぶという。

The ancient city of Bagan, in Myanmar, and home to the world's third largest Buddhist monument. Seemingly countless pagodas, over 3000 of them, are scattered over a vast forest.

P24 ——————

ミャンマーの首都ヤンゴンにある聖地シュエダゴン・パゴダ。たくさんの黄金色に輝く仏像が置かれ、人々は毎日祈りを繰り返す。

The Shwedagon pagoda in Yangon, capital of Myanmar, and a statue of the Buddha, glistening with gold. Devotees come daily to chant their prayers.

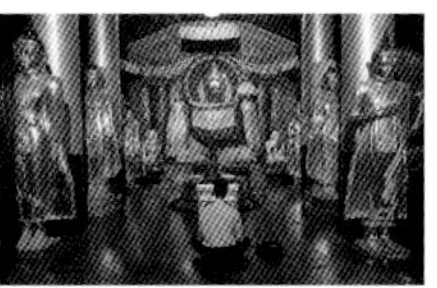

P25 ——————

同じくシュエダゴン・パゴダ。仏陀の聖髪が奉納されたのが始まりで２５００年以上の歴史があると言われている。

Shwedagon Pagoda has been in existence for over 2500 years. It enshrines a lock of hair said to have come from the Buddha.

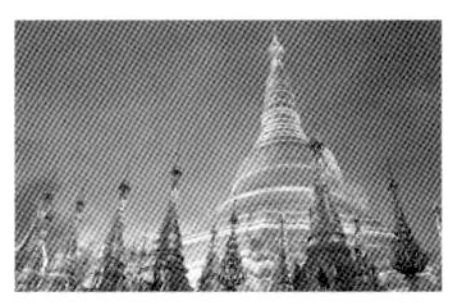

P26 ——————

早朝のシュエダゴン・パゴダ。仏塔の上に広がる鱗雲が幻想的な雰囲気を創りだしていた。

Shwedagon Pagoda in early morning. Scale cloud spread out over the pagoda was to create a fantastic atmosphere.

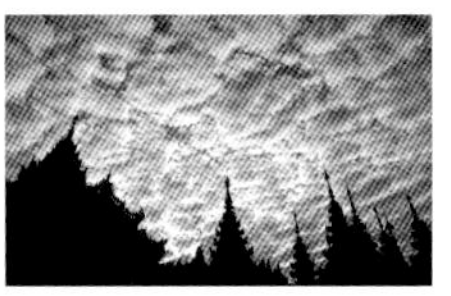

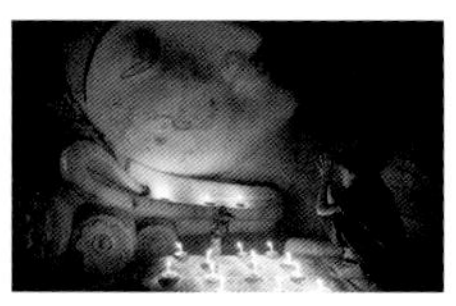

P27 ─────────

寝仏陀の前で祈りを捧げる少年。シィンビンターリャウンという建物の中に納められている寝仏陀で１１世紀頃造られ全長１８ｍある。

Boy praying in front of the reclining Buddha. Are housed in a building that crustacean Shinbinthahlyaung down. This statue, at 18m in length and built around the 11th century.

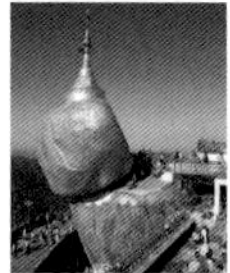

P28 ─────────

ゴールデンロックの名で知られているチャイティーヨー・パゴダ。巡礼地として多くの仏教徒達が訪れる。

Kyaikto Pagoda, also known as Golden Rock Pagoda, is a place of pilgrimage for many Buddhists.

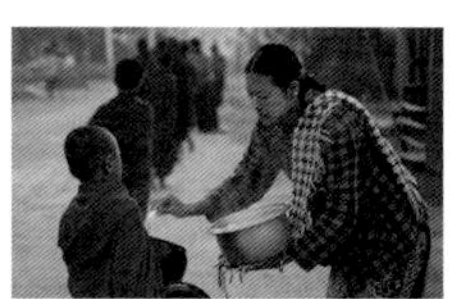

P29 ─────────

朝早く修行僧達は托鉢をしに町を歩き回る。托鉢は仏教徒にとって大切な修行の一つ。

Novice monks roam the town in the early morning, soliciting alms; an essential aspect of preparation for life as a Buddhist monk.

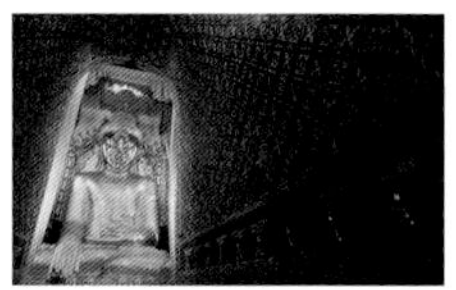

P30 ─────────

ニャウンシュエの町にあるヤダナマンアウン・パヤーという仏塔。

Yadana Man Aung Su Taung Pyay Pagoda in the town of Nyaung Shwe.

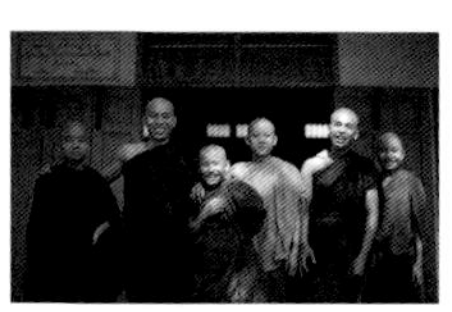

P31 ─────────

アマラプラにある僧院で修行する子坊主達。

Novice monks at a monastery in Amarapura.

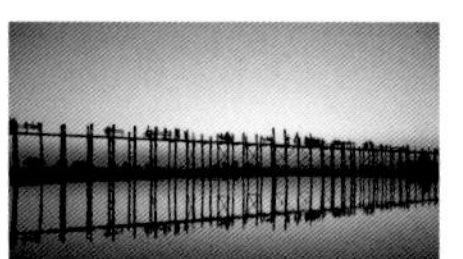

P32,33 ─────────

アマラプラという町にある世界最大級の木造橋ウーベイン橋。全長１２００ｍほどある。この町にはたくさんの寺院があり修行僧達も多く生活している。橋の上で寛ぐ僧達を垣間見る事が出来る。

U Bein Bridge, in the town of Amarapura, is the world's longest teak bridge (1200 m). Amarapura has a large monastery complex housing hundreds of monks and novices, some of whom can be seen relaxing on the bridge.

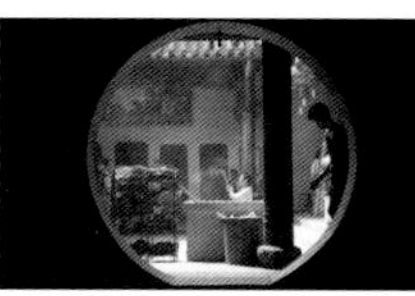

P34 ─────────

観音寺はマレーシアのペナン島にある最古の中国寺院。１８００年代に建てられたもので、中に入ると線香の香りが漂い参拝に訪れる人が絶えない。

Kuan Ying Teng temple is the oldest Chinese temple located on the island of Penang, Malaysia. It was completed in 1800. The scent of incense filters through the interior, lending a special inspiration to the thoughts and meditations of visitors.

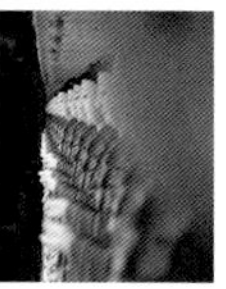

P35 ─────────

ペナン島にあるマレーシア最大の仏教寺院極楽寺では無数の仏像が立ち並ぶ。その数は一万体以上に及ぶという。

Kek Lok Si Temple, on the island of Penang, is the largest Buddhist temple in Southeast Asia . Over 10,000 statues of the Buddha are to found gracing the precincts of the temple.

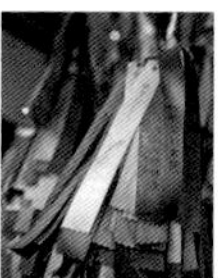

P36 ─────────

極楽寺で飾ってあった願い事や祈りの言葉が書かれた短冊。

Strip wish and prayer that was written in the Kek Lok Si Temple.

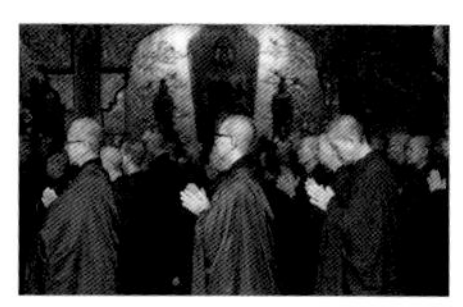

P37 ─────────

極楽寺は１００年以上前に建てられたお寺でたくさんの僧達が暮らし修行している。

Kek Lok Si Temple, built more than 100 years ago, has seen many monks and novices celebrating centuries-old rites and ceremonies.

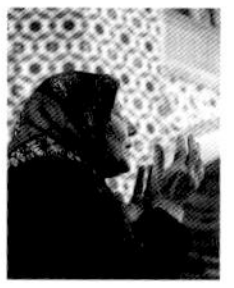

P38 ─────────

タイルの装飾が綺麗な事で有名なモスク、リュステムパシャモスクで祈りを捧げる女性。

Woman praying at the Rüstem Pasha Mosque in Istanbul, famed for its exquisitely beautiful tiled interior.

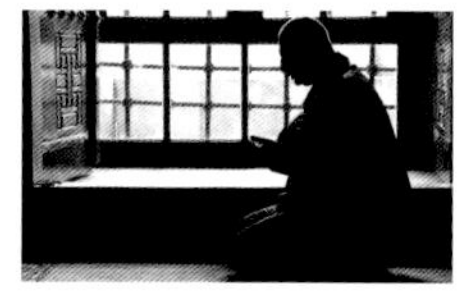

P39 ─────────

トルコのイースタンブールにあるブルーモスクで祈りを捧げるイスラム教徒。

Muslims pray at the Blue Mosque in Istanbul.

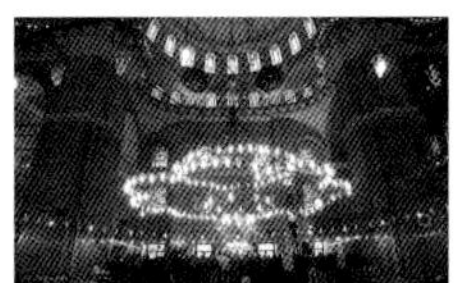

P40

同じくブルーモスクにて。毎日５回の礼拝はイスラム教徒にとっての５行の一つ。他に信仰告白、喜捨、断食、巡礼がある。

Five basic acts are considered obligatory by Islam. Confession of faith, prayer (5 times daily), charity, fasting during Ramadan, and a pilgrimage to Mecca.

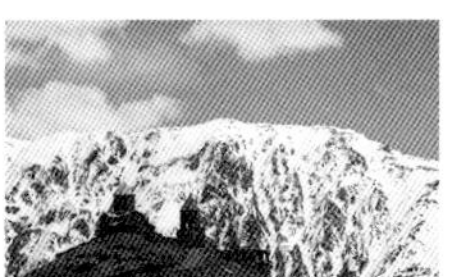

P41

グルジア、カズベキにあるツミンダ・サメバ教会。後ろにそびえ立つのは標高５０３３メートルのカフカス山。

Tsminda Sameba church in Kazbegi,Georgia. directly below Mt. Kazbegi (5,033 m) and other mountains of the Caucasus range.

P42

グルジアのムツヘタにあるスベッティツホベリ大聖堂。11世紀頃現在の石造の教会が再建された。光が差し込む教会内部はとても神秘的な雰囲気が漂っていた。

Svetitskhoveli Cathedral, Mtskheta, Georgia. This cathedral was raised in the 11th century. Inside, the sunlight enhances a mystical sense of a mystery.

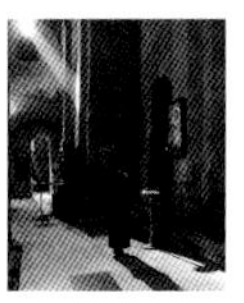

P43

お祈りの前にキリストの絵画にキスをする少女。スベッティツホベリ大聖堂にて。

Before prayer at Svetitskhoveli Cathedral, a young girl kisses an image of Christ.

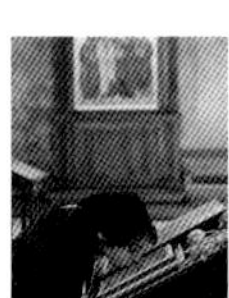

P44

アルメニアの首都イエレヴァンにある聖グリゴール・ルサヴォリッチ教会。アルメニアは３０１年に世界では初めてキリスト教を国教にした国で、信仰深いキリスト教徒がとても多い。

St. Gregory the Illuminator Church in Yerevan, the capital of Armenia. In 301 AD, the ancient kingdom of Armenia became the first nation in the world to adopt Christianity as the state religion. It remains the predominant religion in Armenia.

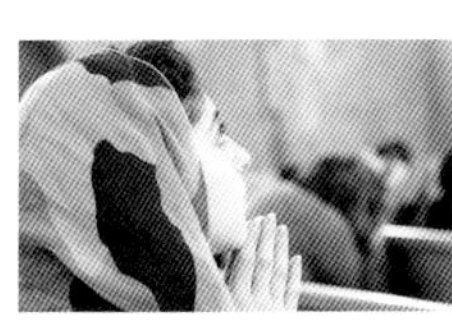

P45

アルメニアにある自称独立国家ナゴルノ・カラバフ。写真はシューシという町にあるガザンチェツォツ大聖堂。未だに戦争の傷跡が残るこの町で行われる日曜日のミサは格別に美しかった。

Ghazanchetsots Cathedral in the town of Shusha, Nagorno-Karabakh, a splinter republic within Armenia. The scars of war against Azerbaijan still remain, however Sunday Mass is an exceptionally beautiful ritual.

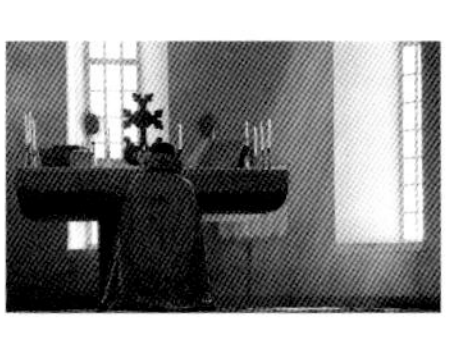

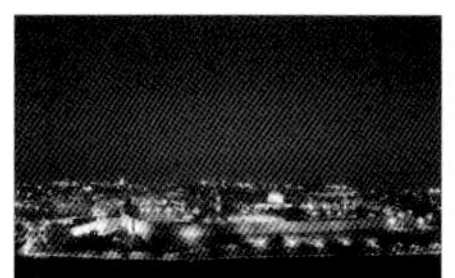

P46

シリアのダマスカスにあるウマイヤドモスク。イスラム教徒にとって４番目の聖地。毎日アザーンが鳴り響き多くのイスラム教徒が礼拝に訪れる。

The Omayyad Mosque in Damascus, Syria. Considered by some Muslims to be the fourth-holiest site in Islam. The Adhan, recited by the muezzin, resounds five times a day, calling the faithful to prayer.

P47

レバノン第２の都市トリポリにあるタイナルモスク。差し込む光の中で熱心にコーランを黙読する青年の姿は神聖な空気が漂っていた。

Taynal Mosque in Tripoli, Lebanon's second largest city. A young man, bathed in sunlight sits silently reading the Koran.

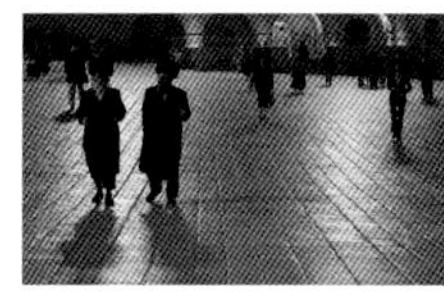

P48,49

日の入り後のエルサレム旧市街。ムハンマドが昇天したといわれている神殿の丘に建つ岩のドームが煌々と輝いている。

The Old City of Jerusalem after sunset. The Dome of the Rock is sparkling in the sunlight, marking the spot where, according to some scholars, Muhammad ascended to Heaven.

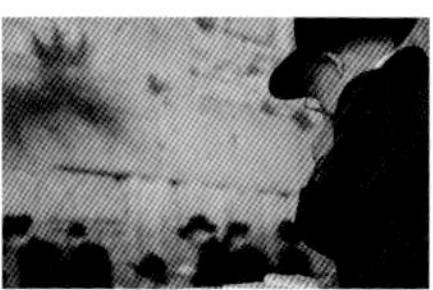

P50

祈りを終え帰路につくユダヤ人。旧市街の中はたくさんのイスラエル兵で警備されていて、常に不安定な状況が続いている。

In the old town, Jews return home after prayers, always within view of numerous Israeli soldiers who keep a constant watch for any sign of trouble. Instability is the only stability.

P51

嘆きの壁の前でユダヤ教経典を朗読するユダヤ人達。大人から子供まで黒のスーツで見にまとった姿は独特の雰囲気を醸し出している。

Jews before the Wailing Wall reading, reciting and chanting prayers. The black dress of adults and children alike give a unique sense of occasion.

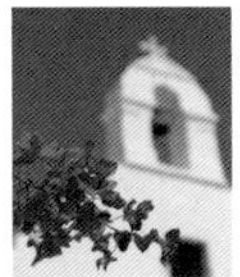

P52 ————

ブーゲンビリアと白亜の鐘楼。白亜の建物と青空が創りだす雰囲気に魅了され、毎年多くの観光客が訪れる。ギリシャのミコノス島にて。

A bell tower in chalk and bougainvillea. The sense of beauty created by the aligning of chalky whiteness of the edifice against a deep blue sky draws many visitors, time and again, to the Greek island of Mykonos.

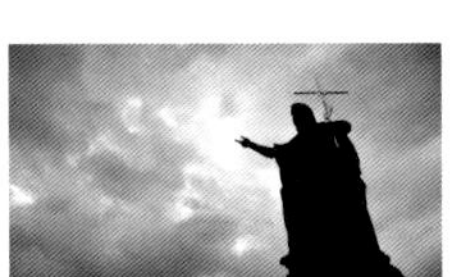

P53 ————

プラハにあるカレル橋。カレル橋の両端には左右に１５体ずつ聖人の彫刻が並んでいる。写真は聖人の一人聖バプティストのヨハネ像。

The Charles Bridge in Prague. At both ends Each side of the bridge is lined with 15 statues of various saints. The depicted image is that of St. John the Baptist.

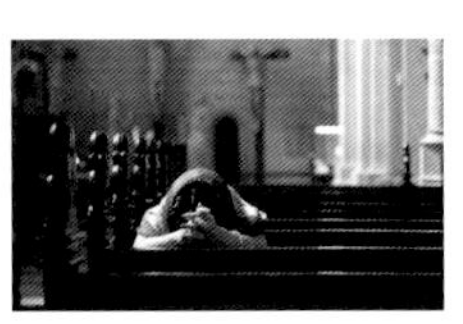

P54 ————

クロアチアの首都ザグレブにある聖母被昇天大聖堂で祈りを捧げるキリスト教徒。

Christians praying in the Cathedral of the Assumption of the Virgin Mary in the Croatian capital of Zagreb.

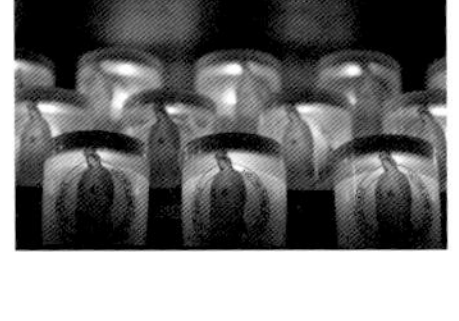

P55 ————

パリにあるノートルダム大聖堂のキャンドル。キャンドルの灯火とステンドグラスが織りなす光の空間はとても幻想的。

A candle in Notre Dame Cathedral, Paris. The flickering candlelight glinting on the stained glass windows. Entrancing, enthralling.

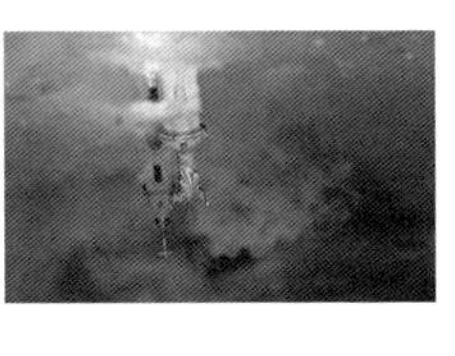

P56 ————

ポルトガルの聖地ファティマにあるキリスト像。この地はファティマの聖母出現と呼ばれる宗教的幻視によって有名になり、今では多くの人が巡礼しに訪れる。不治の病や病気が治癒したりと奇跡が起こる事でも知られている。

Statue of Jesus Christ at the Basilica of Fatima, Portugal. Fatima came to prominence after the appearance of Our Lady of Fatima to three children. A most important destination for pilgrims, a visit to Fatima has also graced with miraculous cures the faithful who may be diseased or incurable.

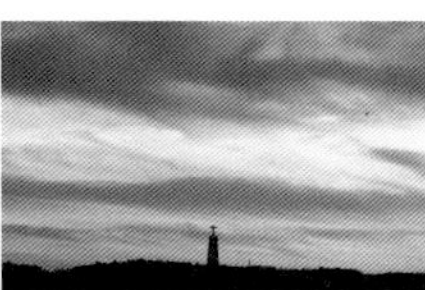

P57 ————

ポルトガルのリスボンにあるカトリックの記念碑クリスト・レイ像。高さ７９ｍある記念碑からはテージョ川をはさんでリスボンの街が一望出来る。

The statue of Cristo Rei, in Lisbon, Portugal. This 79-metre high monument looks over the city of Lisbon across the Tagus River.

P58 ————

ソ連時代この地は何度もソ連軍によって取り壊され、その度に人々が訪れ十字架を置いて祈りを捧げ、今の姿になった。

The site was bulldozed several times by the Russian army during the Soviet era, but then, as now, pilgrims still came to pray and leave a cross after every visit.

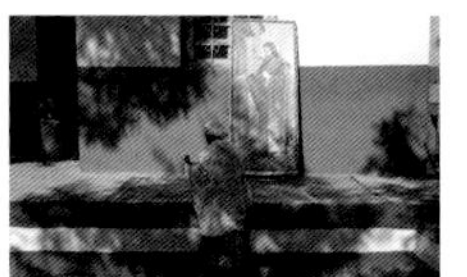

P59 ————

日が沈み静寂に包まれる十字架の丘。無数に浮かび上がる十字架のシルエットが神秘的。

The Hill of Crosses wrapped in silence after sun goes down. The silhouettes of numerous crosses emerge in mysterious, myriad forms.

P60,61 ————

リトアニアのシャウレイという田舎町にある十字架の丘と呼ばれる場所。数万個以上の十字架が置かれている。

The Hill of Crosses, a site of pilgrimage in the rural town of Siauliai, Lithuania. Tens of thousands of crosses have been placed here by Catholic pilgrims.

P62 ————

エチオピアの教会は国旗のカラーを使ったカラフルな所が多い。緑は肥沃な大地、黄色は希望と正義、赤は国民の勇気と情熱を現す。

The colours and emblem of the Ethiopian flag link its people to the Ethiopian Church. The green stripe represents fertile land, the yellow, peace and harmony between various ethnic and religious groups, and the red stripe represents the courage of its people and the blood spilt in defending the nation.

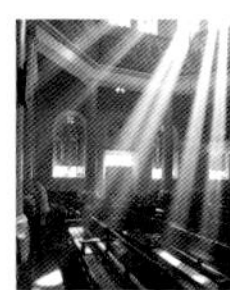

P63 ————

エチオピアの首都アジスアベバにある聖マリア教会。降り注ぐ光が創りだす光景は神秘的な空間を創りだしていた。

St. Mary's Church, Addis Ababa, capital of Ethiopia. A light-filled scene, creating a space where mystery abides.

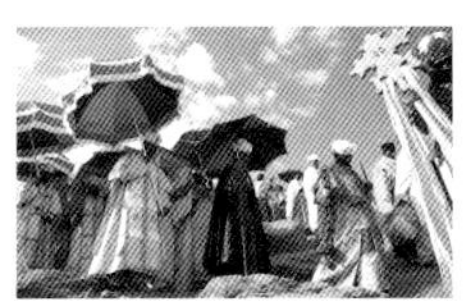

P64 ————————————

エチオピアの聖地ラリベラで行われるティムカット祭。豪華な衣装を身に纏い、司祭達がタボットと呼ばれるモーゼの十戒が納められた棺のレプリカを担ぎ町中を練り歩く。

The Timkat festival held in Lalibela a sacred site in northern Ethiopia. The priests lead a procession around the site, wearing opulent vestments. They bear, on their shoulders a coffer, or tabot, which is a model of the Ark of the Covenant, inside which is placed a replica of Moses' Ten Commandments.

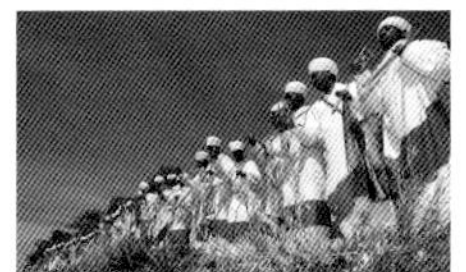

P65 ————————————

お祭りで行われるダンスの1シーン。大勢の人が列を作ったり輪になったりしてシストラムというマラカスの様な楽器を手にし、太鼓や歌に合わせて踊る。

Dancing taking place at the festival. The populace gather together in processions or dance in circles, and play drums, rattle maracas and shake their sistrums.

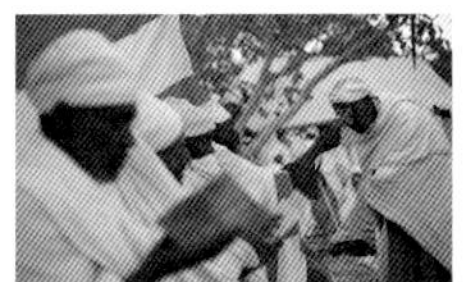

P66 ————————————

司祭から御加護を受ける教徒。エチオピアの国旗の後ろにはタボットが一日安置され、多くの人がここで祈りながら夜を明かす。

The faithful about to receive a blessing from a priest.The tabot is then returned to its sanctuary at the end of the day, and many remain nearby, spending the night in prayer.

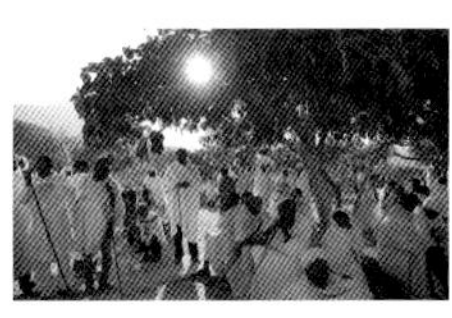

P67 ————————————

タボットが安置される広場の木の下で休む人々。それぞれが祈ったりしながら広場で時間を過ごし司祭やタボットが現れるのを待つ。

Festival-goers rest under a tree in the square near the sanctuary where the tabot will be placed. They pray and wait for the tabot and the clergy to make their appearance.

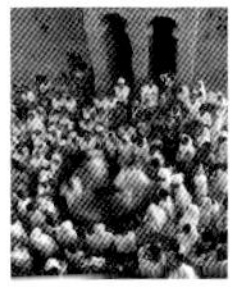

P68 ————————————

石窟教会の前で祝い踊る人々。お祭りの行われる二日間は歌と踊り、そしてお祈りが一晩中続けられる。

Festival-goers dance and rejoice in front of a rock cut church. Singing ,dancing and praying will continue overnight for two days during the festival.

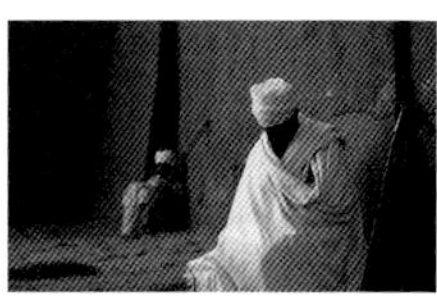

P69 ————————————

石窟教会で休む人々。ほとんどの人々は白い布を巻き付け巡礼にやってくる。

Pilgrims resting on the roof of a rock cut church. Most of those making the pilgrimage are clothed in white.

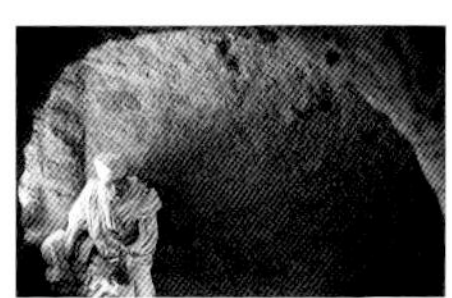

P70 ————————————

石窟教会の中でエチオピア正教の経典を読む老人。

An elder reads out scripture in the church.

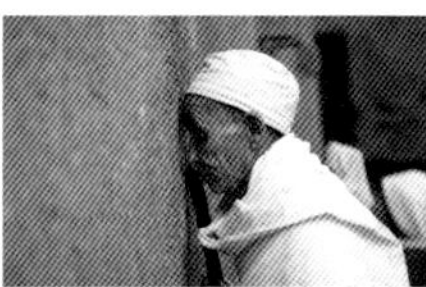

P71 ————————————

石窟教会の壁で祈りを捧げる老婆。

An old woman prays at the wall of the church.

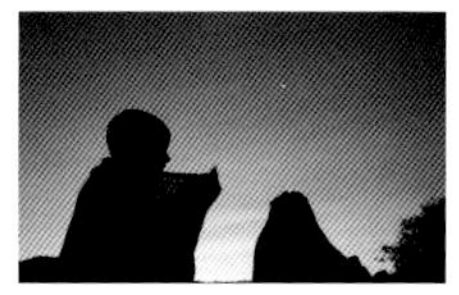

P72 ————————————

タボットが安置されている広場で夜を明かし、祈りながら朝を迎える信者達。

The faithful spend the night in the square by the sanctuary where the tabot is placed and greet the new dawn with prayer.

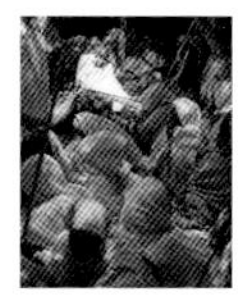

P73 ————————————

同じく広場で夜を明かす人々。夜は冷え込むが寄り添って暖をとっている。

Although it is cold at night, those who spend the night in the square nestle up close to each other to keep warm.

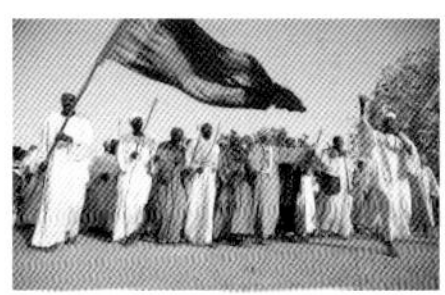

P74 ————————————

スーダンのハルツームでは毎週金曜日スーフィー（イスラム神秘主義）の人達による旋回ダンスの儀式が行われる。

In Khartoum, the whirling dance rituals by Sufi Dervishes (a branch of Islamic mysticism) are performed every Friday.

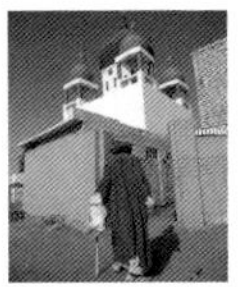

P75 ————————
スーフィーダンスの儀式はハマデルニールモスクの前で繰り広げられる。緑色はイスラム教にとって聖なる色で繁栄を表す。
A Sufi ritual dance is taking place in front of Hamed al-Nil mosque. The color green is holy for Muslims and symbolizes nature, life and purity.

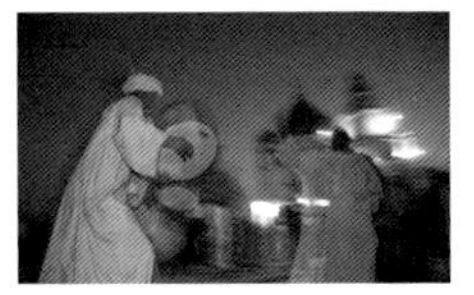

P76 ————————
スーフィーの儀式では香を焚き音楽を奏で、踊ったり旋回したりして神と交信をする。
When Sufis, play music, burn incense and whirl in their dancing they believe that they are communicating with God.

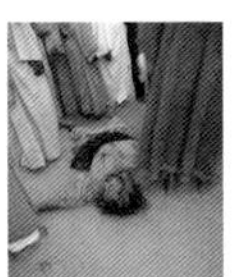

P77 ————————
神との一体化を求め一心不乱に旋回し続け意識を失った信者。こうして旋回を続ける事によって陶酔し雑念を捨て、悟りが開かれるという。この境地に至った者は、時に聖者として認められ崇拝の対象となる。
The believer goes into a trance while continuing to whirl in order to find union with God. While absorbed by constant turning, the follower comes to abandon idle thoughts and their ego and to find "truth". Those who manage to find "perfect truth" are sometimes worshipped and venerated as saints.

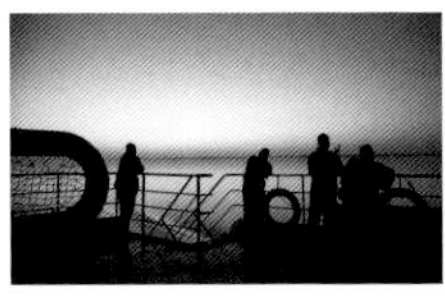

P78 ————————
ナイル川を上ってスーダンからエジプトへ向かう船のデッキで、黄昏時に礼拝するイスラム教徒。彼らはどんな時でもメッカの方角へ毎日5回の礼拝は欠かさない。
Muslims who worship at dusk on the deck of a ship heading from Sudan to Egypt up the Nile. They are required to face Mecca during the 5 daily periods at which they perform their prayer ritual.

P79 ————————
ジャマイカの教会で聖歌を歌う人々。ジャマイカの人達も信仰深く、僕が訪れた普段の日曜日のミサでも市民の人達が涙を流しながら聖歌を熱唱していた。
Churchgoers singing a hymn during a Jamaican Mass. The casual visitor will find that teary-eyed emotion are not unusual at such services.

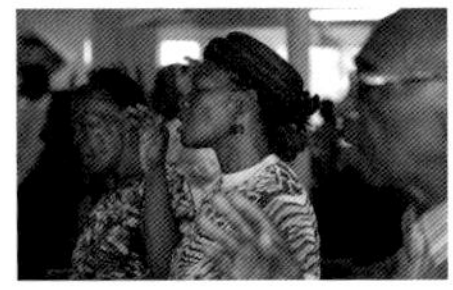

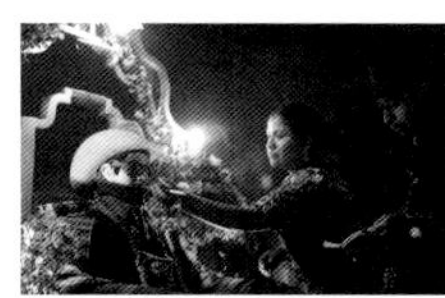

P80 ————————
グアテマラの土着宗教とカトリックが融合してできた密教の神様サンシモン。神様はサングラスをしブーツを履き、人々はお酒とたばこをお供えする。
The god of San Simón is the result of the syncretic fusion of an indigenous Guatemalan religion and Catholicism. This god wears boots and sunglasses, and his followers make him an offering of alcohol and cigarettes

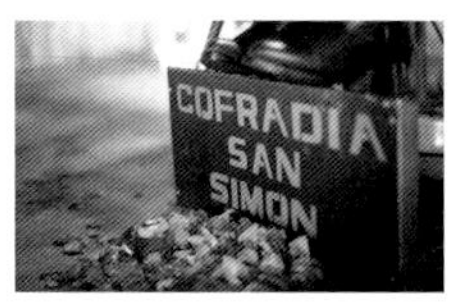

P81 ————————
サンシモンの神様の足下に供えられた花びら。
Petals laid in offering at the feet of the Guatemalen deity, San Simón.

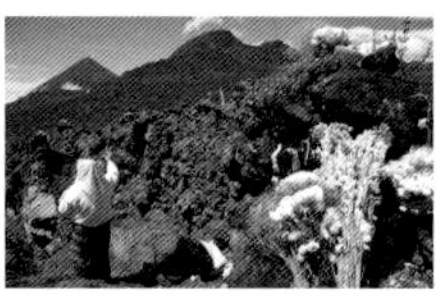

P82 ————————
マヤ人の聖地ムエラ溶岩大地。毎週末マヤの人々はここで幾つかのグループになってお祈りをする。
Muera lava plateau is a holy site for Mayans. They come in small groups to visit and pray every weekend.

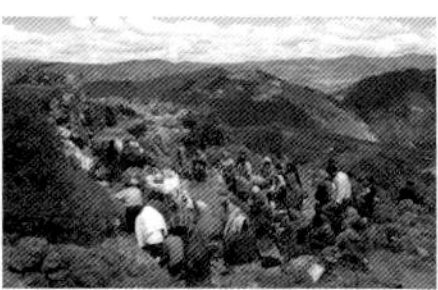

P83 ————————
グループによって祈り方は様々だが、ほとんどのグループはただ祈るのではなく大地に向かって熱唱し、時には拳を突き上げ、泣き叫ぶほど感情を露にして祈りを捧げる。
There are various ways of praying, yet most of these worshippers do not just quietly pray but also energetically direct their chants to nature, sometimes even punching the air with their fists and expressing their feelings emotionally, with tears and loud cries.

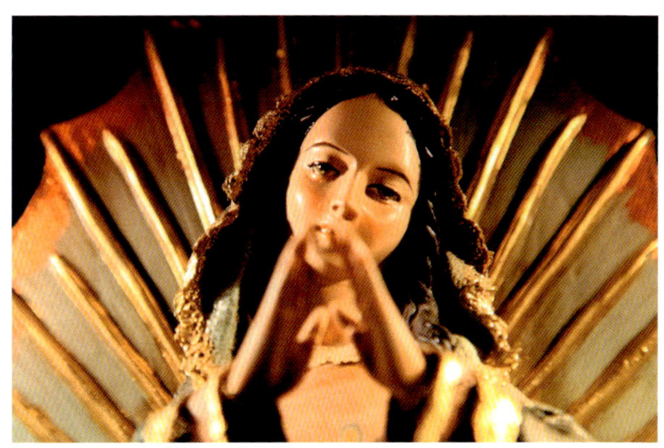

" I dedicate this book for my mother in heaven and all people who I love "

この本を天国の母と愛する全ての人に捧げます。

　僕が祈りをテーマに撮るきっかけとなったのは他ならない母の存在があったからだと思う。というのも、僕が長期の撮影旅行に出かける直前母のガンが再発した。当然、僕は出発を躊躇し思い悩んだ。そんな時背中を押してくれたのは母だった。“後悔しないように行ってきなさい” 僕に一番側に居て欲しかったはずの母が最後に見せてくれた優しさだった。僕は後ろ髪を引かれる想いで日本をあとにした。

　旅が始まり、毎日が新しい発見と刺激、そして出会いの連続だった。毎日が目まぐるしく変わる日々の中でも、僕は母への感謝と病気の回復を願わない日はなかった。母を想う度、僕は自然と寺院や教会など多くの聖地に足を運ぶようになった。そんな時、直向きに祈りを捧げる人達を目にし、僕は純粋に美しいと思った。祈りの対象は違うけれども、真剣な想いは変わらない。どこかで僕は自分の姿を重ね合わせていたのかも知れない。僕は自然と彼らの姿に惹かれていった。と同時に祈りについて考えるようになった。祈りとはなんだろう？人は何故祈るのだろう？何が本当で、何が正しいのか証明出来る人はいないけれども、太古の昔から脈々と受け継がれ信仰され、現在でも世界各地で、また私達の身の周りでも様々な形で残っているのは事実だと思います。それほど祈りというのは私達の生活と密接に関わり、とても重要な行動の一つなのだと思います。当たり前のように身近にあるけれど、その大切さは意外と感じにくい事なのかもしれません。

　また、必ずしも神様に対して行う事が祈りというわけではないと思います。誰かを思ったり、自分が生かされている事を感じ、自然や万物全てに感謝するという事も含めて祈りなのだと思います。しかし、近代化が進むにつれ、祈りの大切さは薄れつつあります。誰もが日々の忙しさに追われ、祈る時間がなくなり、誰もが簡単に何でも手に入る時代になるにつれ、祈る必要性もなくなる。しかし本当にそれでいいのでしょうか？忙しいからこそ、時間を作って毎日を振り返り、見つめ直して、神様や自分自身に問う必要があると思うし、便利な時代だからこそ、そのありがたさを、自然やご先祖様、神様に感謝する必要があるのではないかと思います。この写真集で祈りの素晴しさ美しさに改めて気づいてもらうと同時に神様への感謝、自然への感謝、全ての物事への感謝をするきっかけになれれば意義ある作品になるのではないかと思います。

　最後に、今回撮影させて頂いた方々に心から敬意を表するとともに、この作品を世に送り出して頂きました青菁社の日下部社長、並びに中島氏をはじめご協力頂いたすべての方々、またいつも応援し見守ってくれる家族や友人、妻の沙里に心から感謝したいと思います。

今西 勇人

I can say that it was my mother who made "prayer" the theme of my photography. It was right before I embarked on this long-term photographic journey when my mother's cancer had recurred. That made me hesitate about leaving her for the journey. She never stopped me from leaving however, she would say "Go on the journey, or you will regret it." This was the last kindness I received from my mother, who I believe wanted me, but not anyone else, to stay by her side most. I left Japan with an aching heart.

So my journey began. Everyday I met new people, made new discoveries, and experienced much excitement. Though my days were busy, I never missed a single day to thank my mother and pray for her recovery from cancer. As I thought of her, I realized my feet were spontaneously taking me to many sacred places like churches and temples, where I saw people earnestly praying. I purely thought prayer is beautiful. Although what they pray for is different from religion to religion, they all have the same earnest attitude toward what they are praying for. Maybe I was seeing myself in them. Those people gradually attracted me and made me start to think about the act of praying. What is prayer? Why do we pray? No one can tell what is right and what is true. There is just a fact that the act of praying has been practiced by people from the ancient period, and today it remains in many different forms around the world. Prayer is a very important act and it is closely incorporated into our lives. It is woven into our lives in such a way that sometimes it is hard for us to realize how important it is.

People do not just pray for religious gods or deities. They also pray for someone, and I think even showing respect to nature that we live in or being thankful for all things in this world can be shown in the form of prayer. However, as the world modernizes, we are forgetting how important it is to pray. Living in a busy life, many of us have lost time to pray. Praying has become unnecessary in today's society where we can obtain many things without an effort. But is this how we want it to be? I think we need to look back on our daily lives and talk to our religious deity and yourself all the more because we live in a busy life. We should appreciate living in such a convenient era by thanking nature, our ancestors, and the deity. Through this photo book, I hope people will find prayer to be a wonderful and beautiful act as well as be more thankful for the deity of the religion they practice, nature, and all things around us.

 With the heartiest respect to those who willingly agreed to be in my photos, I would like to show deepest thanks to Mr. Kusakabe, who is the president of Seiseisha and made the publish of this book possible, Mr. Nakajima and all other people who contributed to the book, and my friends and family, especially my loving wife, Sari.

HAYATO IMANISHI

今西勇人 HAYATO IMANISHI

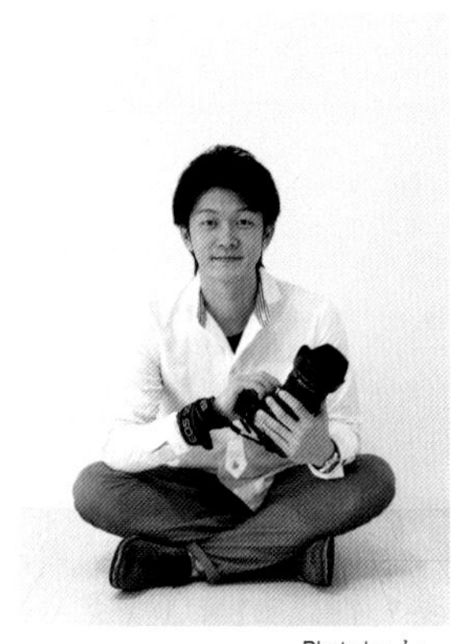

Photo by ムー

１９８１年岐阜県生まれ。大学卒業後、写真スタジオ入社。その後フリーランスに。海外を中心に撮影し各地で個展を開催。これまでに８０カ国以上訪れ、オランダ、マレーシア、南アフリカ、メキシコ、アルメニアなどで写真展を開催。現在国内を拠点に活動中。

Born in 1981 in Gifu prefecture, Japan. He joined a photo studio after graduating from university, then became a freelance. Hayato has been taken a photograph mainly overseas and held a solo exhibition in various country. He has visited more than 80 countries so far and held a photo exhibition in Netherlands, Malaysia, South Africa, Mexico, Armenia. He based in Japan today.

https://www.hayatophoto.com

Voyage of Prayer
— 祈りの旅 —

発行日 —— 2013 年 4 月 22 日　初版 1 刷
著　者 —— 今西勇人
発行者 —— 日下部忠男
発行所 —— 株式会社 青菁社
〒 603-8053 京都市北区上賀茂岩ケ垣内町 89-7
TEL.075-721-5755　FAX.075-722-3995
装丁 , デザイン・乾山工房（日下部忠）/ 印刷・サンエムカラー / 製本・新日本製本
ISBN978-4-88350-174-8
無断転載を禁ずる

Date of Publication —— April 22th,2013
Photography —— Hayato Imanishi
Publisher —— Tadao Kusakabe
Seiseisha Publishing Co.,Ltd.
89-7,Iwagakakiuchi-cho,Kamigamo,Kita-ku,Kyoto 603-8053,Japan
Phone:075-721-5755　Fax:075-722-3995
Art Direction-Kenzan Kobo/Printing-SunM color Co.,Ltd./Book Binding-Shinnihon Bindery Co.,Ltd.
ISBN978-4-88350-174-8
©Hayato Imanishi,2013 Printed in Japan